The Indo

Kitchen

The Indonesian Kitchen

Copeland Marks

WITH

Mintari Soeharjo

NEW YORK

Atheneum

Atheneum
Macmillan Publishing Company
866 Third Avenue, New York, NY 10022
Collier Macmillan Canada, Inc.

Library of Congress Cataloging-in-Publication Data

The Indonesian kitchen.

Includes index.
1. Cookery, Indonesian. I. Marks, Copeland.
II. Soeharjo, Mintari.
TX724.5.I5I56 641.59598 80-23103
ISBN 0-689-70667-7 (pbk.)

Macmillan books are available at special discounts for bulk purchases for sales promotions, premiums, fund-raising, or educational use.
For details, contact:

Special Sales Director
Macmillan Publishing Company
866 Third Avenue
New York, NY 10022

First Atheneum Paperback Printing 1984

10 9

Designed by Kathleen Carey

Printed in the United States of America

Acknowledgments

No book of traditional recipes could possibly be written from an archipelago of three thousand inhabited islands, without the freely given information that derives from the native folk knowledge. We are particularly indebted to Mrs. Rose Siregar, her husband, Manu, and other members of her family who were indispensable in providing many recipes from the island of Sumatra; to Mrs. M. Soemarno of Jakarta who gave us old family recipes from Java; and to members of the various Indonesian offices in New York.

In particular, we should like to express our thanks to Elizabeth Lambert Ortiz for sharing her formidable knowledge of the origins of food plants and their movement from one continent to another.

Contents

The Indonesian Kitchen

INDONESIA
THAILAND
PHILIPPINES
Pacific Ocean
N
South China Sea
Penang
WEST MALAYSIA
Kuala Lumpur
Singapore
Straits of Malacca
BRUNEI
EAST MALAYSIA
Celebes Sea
SUMATRA
KALIMANTAN (BORNEO)
Makasar Strait
HALMAHERA
Molucca Sea
MALUKU ISLANDS
BIAK
BANGKA
SUNDA ISLANDS
Java Sea
CELEBES (SULAWESI)
BURU
SERAM
IRIAN JAYA
Ujung Pandang (Makasar)
Banda Sea
MANOEK
Jakarta
MADURA
Bali Sea
AROE ISLANDS
Indian Ocean
Selat Sunda
JAVA
Surabaya
BALI
LOMBOK
SUMBAWA
KOMODO
FLORES
Flores Sea
WETAR
DAMAR
LETI
Arafura Sea
Savu Sea
TIMOR
SUMBA
SAWOE ISLANDS
NUSA TENGGARA
Timor Sea
Miles
0
200
400
AUSTRALIA
© 1980 A. Karl/J. Kemp

Introduction

Man's insatiable search for spices has become one of the legendary epics of romantic adventure, replete with camel caravans, predatory pirates and Asian inscrutability. Since ancient days the lure has been the Spice Islands in the South China Sea, where vast fortunes could be made—or lost. Indonesia was the site of this mysterious paradise, an archipelago of more than 3,000 islands stretching a distance of 3,000 miles, from Sumatra in the west to the wild coast of New Guinea in the east.

The desire for spices has not abated since biblical times; on the contrary, it has expanded to a degree never dreamed of by the early Arab traders. The United States alone imports more than 292 million pounds of assorted spices and grows more than 100 million pounds per year. The American interest in spices has apparently become inexhaustible. A passion for new culinary sensations has tantalized the American cook. Adventurous cooking is in the air.

To our knowledge, this will be the first cookbook published in the United States and geared to the American kitchen that includes the recipes of native Indonesian cooks from several islands. Many of the recipes have been gleaned from old family records that reflect the authentic knowledge of the different island cultures. Most, as one might expect, are from the two most important islands, Java and Sumatra, with a liberal sprinkling from other well-populated regions.

Ingredients for the most part are now easily found throughout the United States, but perhaps more easily in metropolitan areas where Asian communities are established. The exotic spices, such as salam, laos, kencur and kemiri nuts (see page 12), can be purchased once in modest quantities and need not be renewed for a year or more.

Our book, which we are calling *The Indonesian Kitchen,* is aimed toward the American kitchen so that one of the great cuisines of Asia can be integrated into the repertoire of the American cook. The recipes have been thoroughly tested with the standard American measuring equipment, but our commitment to authenticity within the framework of the tradition has been maintained throughout.

Indonesian cooking is infinitely more varied than the Indian, from which it was derived, it is not as ceremonial as the Japanese, but far spicier and with a greater dimension of flavors, and it is different from the great Chinese cuisine, which exerted an early influence.

The average person knows relatively little about Indonesia and its fascinating cuisine, which boasts of four great external culinary influences: Indian, Chinese, Arabian and Dutch Colonial. Each group contributed something in direct proportion to the length of its influence and the receptivity of the native

Indonesians. The Indonesians have absorbed four foreign cultures, fitted them to the ambiance of an island archipelago and emerged with distinctive and distinguished results.

The cuisine of Indonesia is an onion of many layers, and peeling away a layer to discover the origin of a particular dish can be fascinating. Above all, it is spicy, utilizing those spices native to the fertile islands, plus new ones introduced by successive waves of traders. It is the genius of the Indonesian to incorporate into the cuisine that which he finds in nature, giving it a greater dimension and expanding dining into an aesthetic experience.

Spices were once used to mask the odors of foods that were not fresh. Today refrigeration has solved that problem, but with the advent of artificial fertilizers and other modern agricultural methods, meats, fruits and vegetables no longer have the vivid flavors that nature bestowed on them. Transportation, time lags between the fields and the kitchen, cold storage and preservatives have altered or diluted the flavors to a blandness that must be treated with spices to be attractive.

An insight into Indonesian foods will open up new worlds and expand the horizon of the American kitchen. The use of spices in the unique combinations of this cuisine will restore interest in supermarket foods and supplement the home repertoire of dishes for entertainment or daily dining.

Kitchen Techniques and Equipment

How does one approach a cuisine celebrated in Asia and Holland but relatively unknown and imperfectly understood elsewhere (it is full of hot chilies!) when one has not lived in Indonesia or dined well on the food and when one has no memory of flavors and appearance to assist in assembling the dishes? The answer is simple: Keep cool, don't panic and read each recipe well before embarking on a cooking excursion.

Many of the dishes can be prepared days or even weeks in advance, frozen and then unveiled the day of the fiesta. This is of enormous convenience for a menu that should contain a variety of food in modest quantities, rather than one or two entrées cooked in large amounts.

Cooks who have a working knowledge of Indian or Chinese cooking will have no problem in assembling an Indonesian menu for two or twenty-two. The important consideration is to have on hand the basic list of spices and seasonings (see pages 10–13) and a plan of action for spacing the preparation. Timing is vital to preclude last-minute panic.

The conventional methods of cooking are used, with broiling, steaming, braising, frying and deep frying the most common. The following is a suggested, if not indispensable, assortment of kitchen tools for the most efficient preparation of the recipes:

a. Steamer. A Chinese-style metal steamer with three tiers that will be used for certain rice dishes, for steaming packages of meat or fish and for desserts. In particular, those dishes such as *Nagasari*—Steamed Plantain Dumplings, which are cooked in aluminum foil envelopes, require a steamer for the individual portions.

b. Wok. This Chinese cooking utensil (there are also Indonesian versions) is ideal for deep frying fritters as well as for other dishes that do not require long-time braising. A slotted, long-handled metal spoon is a practical tool to accompany the wok.

c. Electric Rice Cooker. There is nothing wrong with conventional rice cooking methods, but the electric rice cooker has revolutionized the kitchen in Japan and will do the same in the United States.

d. Electric Blender. This is truly indispensable in an era without servants. The very vital preparation of coconut milk (see pages 14–16) and some sauces (bumbu) is most efficiently handled by the blender. Only a masochist would wish to suffer long hours of struggling to cook in the preelectricity Indonesian village manner. Authenticity is not sacrificed by use of a blender.

e. Mortar and Pestle. The round, flat-bottomed stone mortar and pestle called the ulekan (mine is a still-useful antique six inches in diameter) crushes the kemiri nut, garlic, onions, etc. in preparation for a smoother reduction by the blender. In

Indonesia the mortar can be of a large family size that will handle a variety of ingredients crushed into a smooth, liquid paste by the expert. A stone Mexican metate is very similar to the ulekan.

Useful kitchen equipment and sufficient precooking preparation can erase the myth of a difficult cuisine.

Spices and Other Seasonings

The Indonesian way of life, based on an intensive agricultural economy, is close to nature. It is not surprising, therefore, that nature, in the form of spices, has been incorporated into the cuisine.

It is quite possible that no other cuisine dispenses spices with so lavish and loving a hand as the Indonesian. Aromatically extravagant and often fiery hot with pepper and chili, the welding of spices with meat, fish or vegetables is done within a disciplined ancient cooking tradition that belies the extravagance.

Many of the recipes included in this book contain long lists of spices, for example, *Satay Pentŭl*—Meatball Barbecue, which calls for eleven spices in all. A recipe of this type should not intimidate the chef but rather inspire his skill and enthusiasm. The rewards of producing a unique and delicious dish will more than compensate for the additional necessary steps.

Only in the use of the red hot chili does the Indonesian throw caution to the wind and abandon himself to the agony and ecstasy of wrestling with that raging volcano in its many manifestations. But we need not challenge our taste buds or digestive system—use hot chili with prudence!

The following is an annotated list of spices and seasonings which one should have available. Omitting a spice, one of the rare ones, or substituting another may alter the authentic flavor somewhat without totally jeopardizing the recipe. We do not recommend substitutions, but some valid ones are suggested as preferable to doing without.

a. Cinnamon. All the recipes require cinnamon bark.
b. Clove, whole and ground.
c. Coriander, ground.
d. Cumin, ground.
e. Curry powder, any standard popular brand.
f. Chili, or capsicum, either fresh or dried, red or green, hot, mild or sweet.

As Elizabeth Lambert Ortiz observes, "It is universally accepted that all members of the capsicum family, the chili, originated in the Valley of Mexico about 7000 B.C. Once Columbus found chili in Mexico, it spread as the world wanted it." Amazingly adaptable and immediately desirable, the chili spread to many parts of the world. In the fifteenth and sixteenth centuries the chili traveled with the Portuguese and Dutch to Indonesia, where it took hold and became an indispensable ingredient, if not a preoccupation, of their cuisine.

The chili can be treated in several ways to fulfill the requirements of the recipes in this book. Dried, red hot chilies are available in abundance in Spanish-American and Asian food shops. The fresh red and green hot chili, although not always available at all seasons, is ubiquitous, especially in the larger cities in the United States where there are Central American communities.

For purposes of convenience and availability, the dried red hot chili can be used at all times by crushing the whole chili or using the flakes—whichever the recipe or one's tolerance indicates. Soak the dried chili in several teaspoons of water for twenty minutes. This will soften it for blending or otherwise incorporating in the recipe. However, one must always be prepared for the variable pungency of the chili, dried or fresh.

The fresh hot or semihot chili can be prepared in advance by slicing and pulverizing a quantity in a blender with sufficient water to provide lubrication. This simple chili paste can be measured and used as needed. It can also be made in some quantity, let us suggest 1 cup, and refrigerated for several weeks.

The semihot chili which appears in many recipes is my own nomenclature to describe a relatively mild/hot but fresh chili that is found in supermarkets and Asian food shops. It is from 4 to 6 inches in length, with a shiny green or red skin, and is twisted in a corkscrew shape. It may not have the power of the Mexican varieties that are also available fresh, but the semihot is more common and has sufficient heat intensity to fill any requirements. As in all chilis, the seeds and inner connecting tissue have power and so must be taken into account.

The red sweet bell pepper or capsicum provides the red color for sauces such as that in *Telor Bumbu Bali*—Spiced Eggs, Bali style. By blending ½ cup red pepper with the required hot chili, the sauce takes on an attractive rosy hue while retaining the heat level of the recipe.

g. Garlic.

h. Ginger. The fresh ginger root has become so common throughout the United States that there should be no problem at all in obtaining some. I have never used the dry, powdered ginger and do not recommend it.

i. Kemiri nut. The macadamia nut is a legitimate substitute, but we would recommend it be unroasted or roasted but not salted.

j. Kencur—no substitute. We recommend soaking the dry root in a teaspoon or two of water for thirty minutes before using. This process releases the flavor.

k. Jeruk purut, the dried leaf and skin of the citron. One square inch of lemon peel can be substituted.

l. Lemon grass. Dry lemon grass can be found in several forms in Asian food shops. One style is cut horizontally from the root and bulb in ¼-inch pieces and dried. Another type is sold as a stalk of about 8 inches long, and the third is sold in 2- to 4-inch blades. All the recipes call for a stalk of lemon grass, which is equivalent to about a teaspoon of the horizontal stems or five to seven blades of the shorter type. Naturally, the fresh green stalk of lemon grass, which can be grown at home or, occasionally, purchased, is preferable since it brings us one step closer to authenticity.

m. Laos—no substitute. Dried laos root can be purchased in groceries that cater to Southeast Asian cuisines. The laos is packaged in small, thin dried slices, the size of a dime. A recipe, therefore, would require one or more pieces of dried laos. Soak the laos root slices for thirty minutes in ¼ cup water before using.

n. Nutmeg, ground.

o. Onion/shallot. Our recipes call for the supermarket onion since shallots are expensive and no serious deprivation occurs in the substitution. In Indonesia, however, the shallot is used almost exclusively in cooking, while the standard onion, known as the Bombay onion (which reveals its origin), is eaten raw in salads. Should one wish to use shallots, take 4 for each medium-sized onion, or about ¼ cup.

p. Peanut butter, the smooth or crunchy variety, store-bought or homemade.

q. Pepper, white or black, ground.

r. Salam—no substitute. Soak the salam leaf for thirty minutes in ½ cup water before using.

s. Shrimp (sauce) paste. This is a bottled concentrate of shrimp with the consistency of toothpaste which, used in small amounts, gives sauces a greater dimension of flavor. It is found principally in Asian food shops and can be used directly from the bottle without further processing. There is no substitute.

t. Sweet soy sauce, which you can make at home (see page 237).

u. Tamarind. The dark amber or black pulp can be purchased in pressed cakes or in bulk, sometimes containing the fibers and large seeds which resemble a lima bean. One must be prepared for botanical differences in the tamarind which influence its flavor. To use, soak ¼ cup pulp in ½ cup water for one hour, and strain through a metal strainer, discarding the seeds and stringy fibers. The tamarind liquid is what is required in all the recipes; it's the unique acid flavor that throws into focus the other seasonings. I do not recommend a substitute, but sour lemon juice might be an approximation.

v. Turmeric, ground—known as Indian saffron in France. It is the yellow spice found in a standard curry powder.

The Coconut

Coconut milk is an indispensable ingredient of many Indonesian dishes. Without it the natural oil and essence are lost. It adds to the flavor that can be identified as Indonesian; it is the liquid that lubricates the cooking process; it contains vitamins, minerals and protein; it is derived from the coconut meat, the fruit of the coconut palm, often called the tree of life.

Indonesia is one of the world's largest producers of coconuts. The 3,000 or more islands of the archipelago, with their exposure to the sea, are a natural haven for the coconut palm, a tree with a natural affinity for salt water and islands.

The dry coconut, without the fibrous outer husk, is available in many supermarkets and specialty food shops throughout the United States. It is this round object with its hard brown outer shell that interests us in the Indonesian kitchen.

How to Make Coconut Milk and Extract the Meat

1. Take one whole dry coconut, and break it open with a hammer by giving it several hard whacks. Break it into four or five pieces. The liquid that runs out is coconut water.

2. Place the pieces on a gas burner, brown, shell down, directly over the flame for two or three minutes. The heat loosens the meat from the shell. Pry it out with a firm, dull blade, and discard the outer shell. Rinse the meat in cold water, and dry it.

3. Cut the meat into ½-inch pieces. One average coconut should provide 4 to 5 cups of meat. Place 2 cups in a blender with 2 cups of hot water, and blend for two minutes, or until the coconut is broken into coarse grains. The white liquid is the milk, extracted from the meat.

4. Pour the mixture through a metal sieve, and squeeze out as much liquid as possible with your hand. This milk is the first pressing, which is the richest milk or cream. Should you wish to return the coconut residue to the blender, add 1 cup hot water, and blend again; the second pressing will be a diluted milk but still usable. The pulp is then discarded. One coconut will yield 5 to 6 cups of milk.

The coconut milk can be prepared in advance, and in quantity, and stored in the refrigerator for several days. It can also be frozen in containers and used as needed.

Another method of extracting the meat easily from the coconut shell is to bake the whole nut in a 375-degree oven for fifteen minutes. Several sharp whacks with a hammer will then open the nut, and the meat can be extracted easily.

Grated coconut meat is used in many recipes. The meat is extracted as explained in the preceding paragraphs and grated on the medium/fine side of a metal hand grater to produce slender, short fragments. The food processor will also reduce coconut meat to fine slivers. Grating by hand may be tedious, but the size of the coconut fragments it yields is controllable.

Rice

Rice was recorded as a staple crop of China in about 2800 B.C. and in India just a little later. Considering the ancient historical influence of both India and China on the cuisine of Indonesia, we may assume that rice arrived as a staple cereal during that era.

Indonesian rice production averaged from 16 to 17 million tons per year according to the figures of 1978–79. Yet an additional 2.7 million tons must be imported to feed a population of about 135 million spread over a vast archipelago with more than 3,000 inhabited islands, an average of 340 pounds per person per year.

The Indonesians have developed an intensive agricultural economy that is geographically and climatically centered on rice. The cultivated rice terraces of Java and Bali, some centuries old, reflect the mysticism that surrounds the growing of rice. Indonesians believe that rice has a soul like that of a person. Rice fields in bloom are treated with deference like a pregnant woman, and people abstain from firing guns or making loud noises lest the "soul" of the rice miscarry and bear no grain.

In Hindu Bali, where rice is the very basis of life, its growing is presided over by Dewi Sri, the rice goddess. At harvest time, intricate ceremonies are devised for the cutting of the grain.

Indonesians eat rice three times each day and have developed flavored rice dishes for ceremony and for daily living. In addition to the conventional varieties of rice, they use the more glutinous (also known as sweet or sticky) rice, which becomes sweet and sticky after cooking. This type of rice is used in several Asian cultures and is available in all Southeast Asian food shops. In one of the Indonesian wedding rituals, rice is colored with turmeric to give it a golden tinge.

Nasi Kuning
YELLOW RICE
(ALL INDONESIA)

Yellow rice is a ceremonial dish eaten to celebrate happy occasions, such as weddings, wedding anniversaries, birthdays and the birth of children.

- 1 *cup rice*
- 1¾ *cups coconut milk* (*see page 15*)
- 1 *stalk lemon grass*
- 2 *salam leaves*
- ¼ *teaspoon turmeric*

½ teaspoon salt

Aluminum foil

1. Wash the rice in cold water several times, and drain. Add the rice to the coconut milk and all the other ingredients, and bring to a boil in a saucepan. Cook, covered, over low heat for ten minutes, or until the liquid is absorbed by the rice.

2. Place the partially cooked rice on aluminum foil in a Chinese-style steamer, and steam for twenty minutes over medium heat. Serve hot or at room temperature.

Serves 4, with other dishes

Lontong
RICE ROLLS
(ALL INDONESIA)

Lontong *is a traditional food that travels well. Wrapped in banana leaves and eaten at picnics or in the home, it is the quintessential Indonesian food of the country. The* Lontong *would be an extremely useful dish to perfect for the modern kitchen. It can be made several days in advance and refrigerated until needed. It can be eaten either warm or cold and then warmed again by covering the rolls with water and boiling for ten minutes. The rolls freeze well but must be thawed for several hours before reheating.*

1 cup rice

3 cups water

6 pieces aluminum foil, each 12 inches square

1. Rinse the rice in cold water several times, and drain. Cook the rice and water, covered, for fifteen minutes over medium heat. Remove the covered saucepan from the heat, and allow the water to be absorbed and cool for fifteen minutes more.

2. To make the rice rolls, place 1 cup cooked rice near the edge of a foil square. Pat the rice firmly into a sausage shape 6 inches long and 1½ inches in diameter. Roll the foil over one turn, and seal the ends, always keeping the rice firmly against the foil. Continue to roll a complete turn, and seal the ends tightly.

3. Place the rolls in boiling water to cover, cook for one hour.

4. Drain, and allow the rolls to cool for one-half hour so that they can be handled easily. Open the foil, and cut the roll into ½-inch-thick slices.

Makes 6 rolls

Nasi Uduk
RICE COOKED IN COCONUT MILK
(JAVA)

Partially cooking rice in conventional style and then completing the cooking in a steamer are a typically Indonesian method of obtaining individual rice grains perfectly steamed. The Nasi Uduk *or any other rice dishes that are prepared by this twice-cooked method may also be cooked to completion according to one's own conventional method.*

2 cups rice
3 cups coconut milk (see page 15)
1 salam leaf
½ teaspoon salt

Aluminum foil square

1. Put all the ingredients into a saucepan, and bring to a boil. Turn off the heat, cover the pan and let the mixture stand for fifteen minutes to allow the rice to absorb the coconut milk.

2. Place the rice on an aluminum foil square in a Chinese-style steamer. Steam for twenty minutes to complete the cooking.

Serves 8, with other dishes

Nasi Goreng Istimewa
SPECIAL FRIED RICE
(SUMATRA)

Fried rice is one of those well-known Chinese inventions that have made the rounds into banality. The Indonesians have elevated this dish into an event by adding a medley of flavors, decorative garnishes and enough substance so that it might be a meal in itself. The following are two varieties of fried rice, one from the island of Sumatra and the other from Java.

- 1 *egg, beaten with ¼ teaspoon salt and ¼ teaspoon pepper*
- ¼ *cup thin-sliced onion*
- 3 *cloves garlic, sliced thin*
- 2 *tablespoons butter*
- ½ *cup small shrimp, peeled and deveined*
- 1 *cup boneless chicken, cut into ½-inch cubes*
- 2 *teaspoons fresh red hot chili, blended into a paste*
- 2 *teaspoons soy sauce*
- ½ *teaspoon salt*
- 4 *cups cooked rice, slightly undercooked and cooled*

1. Fry the egg into a large, thin omelet. Cut it into thin strips, and set aside.

2. Fry the onion and garlic in the butter in a wok or a large frying pan for about two minutes. Add the shrimp and chicken cubes, and continue to fry for two minutes more. Add the hot chili, soy sauce and salt, and mix well. Then add the rice, and stir well for about five minutes more. The rice should be dry with the individual grains separated.

3. Serve the rice warm or at room temperature on a large open platter. Garnish with the sliced omelet, crispy onions and any type of fritter (pages 203–223); decorate the edges of the plate with red and green sweet pepper flowers and/or tomato flowers (see below). As another option, the rice is occasionally served with one fried egg for each person and generally with a variety of *krupuk* (see page 203).

4. To give the rice a rosy, pink color, crush the hot chili with some ripe tomato, add this mixture to the shrimp and chicken cubes in the wok, and continue as indicated.

Note: To make the pepper flowers, slice the pepper into 12 long, slender strips from the tip to the stem end to form the petals. Carefully remove the inner seeds, and discard. If desired, fill the interior with a mixture of small cubes of cucumber and chopped onion. Both red and green peppers should be used to add color to the rice.

The tomato flower is made in essentially the same manner by cutting the skin into 6 sections from the tip to the stem end. Scoop out the center pulp and seeds, and discard, leaving enough of the outer flesh so that the flower will retain its shape. Fill the center with a cucumber and onion mixture.
Serves 10

Nasi Goreng
FRIED RICE
(JAVA)

- 2 *eggs, beaten*
- 3 *tablespoons peanut or corn oil*
- 1 *teaspoon dried or fresh red hot chili*
- 1 *clove garlic*
- ¼ *cup raw, boneless chicken, cut into bite-size pieces*
- ½ *cup raw shrimp, cut into bite-size pieces*
- 2 *cups cooked rice, cold* Long grain
- ½ *teaspoon salt*
- 1 *tablespoon sweet soy sauce* (*see page 237*)
- 2 *scallions, sliced thin*

1. Fry the eggs in 1 tablespoon of the oil to make one flat omelet. Allow to cool, and slice into thin strips.

2. Crush the chili and garlic together into a paste. Put the remaining 2 tablespoons of oil in a wok or large frying pan, and fry the chili/garlic paste for one minute. Add the chicken and shrimp, fry for another minute and add the rice. Stir well for several minutes, and add the salt, sweet soy sauce and scallions. Stir well, and turn out on a platter. Garnish with the egg strips. A complete and traditional dinner would include the fried rice, *Krupuk* and the *Acar Kuning*—Pickled Vegetable Salad.

Serves 6, with other dishes

Lemper

SWEET RICE-STUFFED ROLL

(JAVA)

Lemper *is an appetizer or snack for the cocktail hour. Exotic and delicious, it gratifies the skill of the cook, the eye of the beholder and the taste buds of the diner. In Indonesia, banana leaves are used instead of aluminum foil to wrap and store the rice rolls, thus imparting a fresh garden flavor.*

2 *cups sweet* (*glutinous*) *rice*
2 *cups coconut milk*
1 *salam leaf*
½ *teaspoon salt*

1. Wash the rice in cold water several times, and drain. Bring the coconut milk, rice, salam and salt to a boil, and remove the saucepan from the heat. Let it stand, covered, for

thirty minutes. Remove the rice, place it on a piece of aluminum foil and steam in a Chinese-style steamer over hot water for thirty minutes. Allow the rice to cool.

2. CHICKEN FILLING

¾ cup boneless raw chicken, cut into small pieces
¼ cup coconut milk (see page 15)
1 teaspoon coriander
2 cloves garlic, sliced
1 teaspoon sugar
2 teaspoons peanut or corn oil
1 teaspoon salt
1 piece of jeruk purut, or 1 square of lemon peel (see page 12)
1 salam leaf

Combine the chicken and coconut milk, and blend into a coarse, grainy mixture. Grind together the coriander, garlic and sugar, and fry in the oil for one minute. Then add the chicken, salt, jeruk purut and salam. Fry for about five minutes, or until the chicken is light brown and dry. Discard the jeruk purut and salam.

3. BEEF FILLING

1 teaspoon coriander
2 cloves garlic, sliced
1 teaspoon sugar
2 teaspoons peanut or corn oil
¾ cup ground beef
1 piece of jeruk purut, or 1 square of lemon peel (see page 12)
1 salam leaf
1 teaspoon salt
¼ cup coconut milk (see page 15)

Grind together in a mortar the coriander, garlic and sugar, and fry for one minute in the oil. Add the beef, jeruk purut, salam, salt and coconut milk. Cook over medium heat for about five minutes, or until the beef is lightly browned. Discard the jeruk purut, salam and any liquid that may have accumulated.

4. THE RICE ROLL

1 cup cooked sweet rice
½ cup beef or chicken filling

two 14-inch squares of aluminum foil

Place half the rice in the center of a foil square, and flatten it out with your fingers into a 4″ x 6″ rectangle about ¼ inch thick. The rice is sticky, and the process will be easier if you cover your fingers with oil. Spread half the beef or chicken filling along the center of the rice rectangle from end to end. Then fold both sides of the foil toward each other, lengthwise, pressing firmly into a roll about 2 inches in diameter. Seal the foil ends to make a firmly packed roll. Repeat with the remaining ingredients to make a second roll.

The rice rolls can be served immediately or refrigerated for up to two days before serving. Remove the rolls from the foil, and slice into 1-inch-thick pieces like a jelly roll. This dish should be eaten at room temperature.

Serves 6 to 8, with other dishes

۞

Nasi Kebuli

LAMB AND RICE, "MAY YOUR WISHES COME TRUE"

(JAVA)

Arab traders have visited the islands of Indonesia since ancient times, searching for spices. The spread of Islam to Indonesia began in the ninth century A.D., *and by the fifteenth century it had gradually eclipsed the Hindu and Buddhist empires. All the islands, with the paramount exception of Bali, which remained Hindu, embraced the Moslem religion. One of the ceremonial dishes of Arab origin, which came to Indonesia via India, venerated the Prophet Mohammed by cooking lamb and rice. Wealthy families distributed the dish to the poor. The lamb buried in the rice, I am told, was a surprise that resulted in one's wishes being gratified.*

½ cup water
1 teaspoon sugar
2 teaspoons salt
3 cloves garlic, sliced
¼ cup sliced onion
2 tablespoons curry powder
3 pounds boneless lamb, cut into 2-inch cubes
2 salam leaves
5 pieces of jeruk purut, or 5 square inches of lemon peel (see page 12)
5 cups coconut milk (see page 15)
4 cups rice, rinsed well in cold water
1 cup reserved lamb sauce

Aluminum foil

1. In a blender, make a paste of the water, sugar, salt, garlic, onion and curry powder. Put the lamb in a large saucepan, and pour this sauce over it. Cook for ten minutes over medium heat; then add the salam, jeruk purut and 2 cups of the coconut milk. Cook for about one hour or more, or until the lamb is soft. There should be about 1 cup of sauce remaining in the pan; reserve it.

2. In a large saucepan, combine the rice with the reserved lamb sauce and the remaining 3 cups coconut milk. Bring to a boil, and stir several times. Turn off the heat, cover the pan and allow the rice to absorb the liquids for fifteen minutes. Place the rice on a square of aluminum foil in a Chinese-style steamer, and steam for twenty minutes to complete the cooking.

3. To serve, put the lamb in the center of a large serving platter, and cover it completely with a mound of the steamed rice.

Serves 8, with other dishes

❁

Nasi Golong
ROUND RICE BALLS
(JAVA)

Round rice balls are a decorative, ceremonial dish prepared for special occasions.

3 cups cooked rice

three 12-inch squares aluminum foil

Place 1 cup of the rice in the center of each foil square, and fold into a ball roughly 4 to 5 inches in diameter. To serve, unfold the foil, and place the rice balls on a serving platter. They are eaten at room temperature.
Serves 6, with other dishes

The Barbecue and Its Sauces

The *satay* is the classic Indonesian barbecue in its many startling manifestations. The barbecue is perhaps man's earliest method of cooking. Possibly, in primitive barbecues, haunches of wild game were suspended over a fire to char. This first barbecue became more refined as the pieces on the stick became smaller until they were reduced by the more fastidious to ½-inch cubes of meat threaded on thin-carved bamboo skewers.

Every island in the Indonesian archipelago has its own style of preparing the *satay,* its own marinade and seasonings to influence the flavor of shrimp, fish, chicken, beef and lamb. The Hindu Balinese favor pork *satay,* which is forbidden on the other, Islamic islands. And all *satays* are most frequently served with a rich thickened peanut sauce, either sweet or hot or both.

If a charcoal grill is unavailable, the *satays* can be broiled in a gas or electric oven. To protect the wooden skewers from burning in the oven, wrap the ends in aluminum foil, or soak the entire skewer for several hours before threading the *satay* ingredients.

❁

Asam Manis
BEEF SATAY IN SWEET AND SOUR FLAVOR
(ALL INDONESIA)

The standard and probably most popular varieties of satay *are those made with chicken and beef. Classically, they are marinated in richly seasoned ingredients or simply spiced and then broiled over charcoal. But the ingredient that influences the flavor most is the peanut sauce into which the cooked* satay *is dipped when eaten, and this can run the gamut from the very sweet favored by the Javanese to the flaming hot favored by the people of Sumatra, with variations of sweet/hot in between. Personal preference tells us everything. All the broiled meat* satays *in this chapter are eaten with the* Sambal Kacang-*Peanut Sauce, found on page 238.*

2 teaspoons coriander
¼ teaspoon ground cumin
2 cloves garlic, crushed
1 teaspoon salt
1 tablespoon light or dark brown sugar
1 teaspoon tamarind, dissolved in 1 tablespoon water
1 pound sirloin or flank steak, cut in 1-inch cubes

THE DIP:

2 tablespoons sweet soy sauce (see page 237)
1 tablespoon water
1 tablespoon peanut or corn oil

Bamboo skewers

1. Crush together the coriander, cumin, garlic, salt, sugar and tamarind liquid, and rub the paste into the cubes of beef. Marinate for one hour at room temperature.

2. Combine the dip ingredients. Put 4 cubes of beef on each skewer, dip into the sauce and broil over charcoal or in the oven for three minutes on each side.

Ayam Ponorogu
CHICKEN SATAY
(ALL INDONESIA)

1 whole breast of chicken, cut into 1-inch cubes

The cubes of chicken can be treated the same way as the sweet and sour beef *satay* above. A simpler method is to marinate the chicken in the dip sauce for thirty minutes and then broil it over charcoal. Still another variation is to salt and pepper the chicken to taste, to dip it into the broiling dip, then to place it over the charcoal. There are variations on variations, and all of them, from region to region, have their enthusiasts, but the sweet-and-sour-flavored *satay* is the favorite in my kitchen.

Serves 4, with other dishes

Satay Terik Ati Ayam

CHICKEN LIVER BARBECUE

(JAVA)

***2** kemiri nuts, crushed*
***¼** cup sliced onion*
***1** clove garlic, sliced*
***½** teaspoon coriander*
***⅛** teaspoon turmeric*
***½** teaspoon salt*
***1** teaspoon sugar*
***¼** teaspoon shrimp (sauce) paste (see page 13)*
***2** dried or fresh red hot chilies, crushed*
***1** cup coconut milk (see page 15)*
***¾** pound chicken livers, separated into lobes*
***2** salam leaves*
***1** piece of laos*

Bamboo skewers

1. Blend into a paste the kemiri, onion, garlic, coriander, turmeric, salt, sugar, shrimp paste, chili, and ¼ cup of the coconut milk. Mix the paste with the chicken liver, and let it stand for fifteen minutes.

2. Put the balance of the coconut milk (¾ cup) into a frying pan, and bring it to a boil. Add the livers, salam and laos. Cook for ten minutes or a bit more, or until almost all the sauce has evaporated. Put 3 sections of the livers on each skewer, and broil over charcoal or in the oven for five minutes, turning

once. To protect the skewers from burning, cover the ends with aluminum foil.

Variation: The cooked livers can also be served with the reduced coconut sauce simply by eliminating the broiling step.
Serves 6, with other dishes

Satay Sapit
CLIPPED BEEF BARBECUE
(JAVA)

This barbecue is traditionally served at the Slametan, *or ceremonial prayer for remembrance of the dead. It is called clipped beef because the bamboo skewers are cut halfway down the center. The pieces of beef are pushed in and held, or clipped, by the forked sticks. Then the skewers are wrapped in banana leaves and put on a charcoal fire to broil.*

- 2 cloves garlic, sliced
- ¼ cup sliced onion
- 2 kemiri nuts, crushed
- 1 teaspoon coriander
- ⅛ teaspoon ground cumin
- ⅛ teaspoon turmeric
- ½ pound sirloin or flank steak, cut into 2-inch cubes
- ½ cup water with ½ teaspoon salt
- 1 salam leaf
- 1 piece laos

1 tablespoon peanut or corn oil
1 teaspoon tamarind, dissolved in 1 tablespoon water
2 tablespoons coconut milk (see page 15)
½ teaspoon salt
½ teaspoon sugar

Bamboo skewers

1. Crush together in a mortar or blender the garlic, onion, kemiri, coriander, cumin and turmeric to make a paste.

2. Cook the beef cubes in the water for ten minutes with the salam and laos. Remove the beef, and discard the liquid. Pound the pieces of beef to flatten them a bit.

3. Fry the spice paste in the oil for one minute over medium heat. Add the tamarind liquid, coconut milk, salt and sugar and then the beef, stirring rapidly to coat the cubes with the seasonings. Continue to cook for a few minutes more, or until all the liquid has evaporated. Put 2 pieces of beef on each skewer, and broil for one minute on each side.

Serves 4, with other dishes

Satay Pentul
MEATBALL BARBECUE
(CENTRAL JAVA)

3 cloves garlic, sliced
¼ cup sliced onion
1 tablespoon coriander
½ teaspoon ground cumin
1 teaspoon tamarind, dissolved in 1 tablespoon water
½ teaspoon pepper
¼ teaspoon nutmeg
⅛ teaspoon ground cloves
¼ teaspoon turmeric
1 slice ginger root (1 teaspoon)
2 cups coconut milk (see page 15)
1½ pounds ground beef
2 eggs, beaten
2 teaspoons salt
1 stalk lemon grass
1 1-inch cinnamon stick
1 tablespoon sugar

Bamboo skewers

1. Crush together in a blender the garlic, onion, coriander, cumin, tamarind liquid, pepper, nutmeg, cloves, turmeric and ginger with ½ cup of the coconut milk. Mix three-quarters of

the spice paste with the ground beef, eggs and salt. Shape this into about 24 egg-shaped ovals, and set aside.

2. Mix the remainder of the spice paste and the remaining coconut milk (1½ cups) with the lemon grass, cinnamon stick and sugar. Bring to a boil in a large frying pan, add the meatballs and cook for five minutes, turning once carefully. The meatballs at this stage are about half done. Remove them from the sauce, and spear 2 on a bamboo skewer. Place the skewers over a charcoal fire or gas broiler, baste with a small amount of the coconut sauce and broil for five minutes, turning once.

Variation: Another method of preparing the *satay*, and one that I have found infinitely satisfying, is to leave the meatballs in the sauce and continue cooking them to completion, basting frequently. The sauce will be reduced by half and will take on a more concentrated medley of flavors. Eliminating the actual touch of flame may not be completely authentic, but it is a more pragmatic approach for the American kitchen that does not have barbecue facilities, and it does not significantly alter the flavor.

Serves 6, with other dishes

Satay Daging Giling
GROUND BEEF BARBECUE
(JAKARTA)

This simple satay, *easy to prepare and with only a light Indonesian touch of spice, could very well replace the ball park style of hamburger.*

1 pound ground beef
½ teaspoon ground cumin
2 teaspoons coriander
¼ teaspoon pepper
1 clove garlic, crushed
1 tablespoon chopped green sweet pepper
1 tablespoon chopped onion
¼ teaspoon sugar
1 teaspoon salt
1 egg, beaten

Bamboo skewers

Mix all the ingredients together. Form the beef mixture into football-shaped kabobs 2 inches long and 1 inch thick. Put 2 kabobs on each skewer, and broil over charcoal or in a gas or electric broiler for about ten minutes, turning several times.
Serves 6, with other dishes

Satay Padang
WEST SUMATRA BARBECUE

This barbecue is a celebrated dish of the city/province of Padang in West Sumatra. There is a Padang expression stating that when food is really good, you would never notice your mother-in-law should she be passing by, the implication being that the food commands all your attention and that your nose would be centered on the plate, ignoring anything else around.

½ cup sliced onion
5 cloves garlic, sliced
3 tablespoons peanut or corn oil
2 veal or beef hearts, quartered
2 pounds beef chuck, cut into 4-inch chunks
1½ pounds veal tongue, cut into 3 pieces
1 pound beef tripe, cleaned and cut into 4 pieces
2 tablespoons fresh red hot chili, blended into a paste
2 tablespoons salt
1 tablespoon turmeric
1 tablespoon fine-chopped ginger
1½ tablespoons coriander
1 teaspoon ground cumin
3 pieces of jeruk perut, or 3 square inches of lemon peel (see page 12)
2 salam leaves
1 piece of laos
1 2-inch cinnamon stick
1 cup water
2 stalks lemon grass
3 cups coconut milk (see page 15)

THE SAUCE:

2 cups coconut milk (see page 15)
1 cup rice flour
Reserved meat sauce
2 teaspoons salt
½ ripe tomato, sliced thin

Bamboo skewers

1. Fry the onion and garlic lightly in the oil in a large saucepan. Add all the other ingredients except the coconut milk, and mix well. Cook, covered, for about one and one-half hours, or until the meats are soft. Then add the coconut milk, and cook for thirty minutes. Remove the meats, and reserve the sauce, which should measure about 2 cups.

2. To make the sauce, mix the coconut milk and rice flour into a thin paste. Bring the reserved meat sauce to a boil, and add the rice flour paste, salt and tomato. Cook, stirring, for ten minutes over a low flame until the sauce is well mixed. If it becomes too thick, add ½ cup water during the cooking. The result should be a thick, creamy, spicy sauce. Keep warm.

3. Cut all the cooked meats into ½-inch cubes. Put 5 cubes of different meats on each skewer so that you have a contrast in textures. Heat the skewer briefly over a charcoal fire, gas or electric broiler; then dip it liberally into the warm rice sauce. The *satays* are usually eaten with rice rolls (page 19). *Serves 10, with other dishes*

Satay Asam Manis Kambing

SWEET AND SOUR LAMB BARBECUE

(SUNDA, EAST JAVA)

The combination of tamarind, sugar and sweet soy sauce in the marinade is irresistible. A most popular method of seasoning lamb for the barbecue.

- 2 *cloves garlic, sliced*
- ¼ *cup sliced onion*
- 1 *teaspoon ground cumin*
- 2 *teaspoons tamarind, dissolved in 1 tablespoon water*
- 1 *tablespoon sugar*
- ½ *teaspoon salt*
- 2 *tablespoons sweet soy sauce* (*see page 237*)
- 1 *pound boneless lamb, cut into 1-inch cubes*
- 1 *tablespoon peanut or corn oil*

Bamboo skewers

1. In a mortar or blender, grind the garlic, onion, cumin, tamarind liquid, sugar, salt and sweet soy sauce into a paste. Mix this with the lamb cubes, and marinate for thirty minutes.

2. Add the oil to the lamb, and mix well. Put 3 or 4 cubes of lamb on each skewer, and broil over charcoal or in the oven for about three minutes on each side. If you are using an electric or gas broiler, it would be prudent to cover the handles of the skewers with aluminum foil to prevent burning.

Serves 6, with other dishes

❁

Satay Panggang Udang Brebes
MARINATED SHRIMP BARBECUE
(CENTRAL JAVA)

Brebes is a town in Central Java where this satay *is reputed to have originated.*

- *2 tablespoons water*
- *1 teaspoon salt*
- *1 teaspoon sugar*
- *1 tablespoon lemon juice*
- *2 fresh green or red semi-hot chilies, sliced*
- *¼ cup sliced red sweet pepper*
- *¼ teaspoon shrimp (sauce) paste (see page 13)*
- *2 cloves garlic, sliced*
- *1 pound raw shrimp, peeled and deveined*

Bamboo skewers

1. Blend the water, salt, sugar, lemon juice, chilies, sweet pepper, shrimp paste and garlic into a smooth paste.
2. Marinate the shrimp in the paste for fifteen minutes. Put 3 shrimp on each skewer, and broil over charcoal or in a gas broiler for five minutes, turning once. Cover the shrimp with a little marinade paste during this process.

Serves 6, with other dishes

Family-Style Soups and Noodles

Indonesian soups are prepared in many ways. Some have a number of separate ingredients which are added in layers to the individual serving bowls and covered with a spiced broth, others are simple in form and are eaten as an accompaniment to the meal.

Noodle dishes have a festive air when prepared for large groups. Although the noodle may be Chinese in origin, it has been incorporated into the Indonesian cuisine as though it had always been there.

Soto Ayam

EAST JAVA CHICKEN SOUP

Soups of many types are favored by Indonesians of all the islands. They are nourishing, filling, beautiful to look at, and the flavors can be controlled by the individual diner who may select a variation in the texture or pungency simply by supplementing his or her individual portion from the variety of help-yourself ingredients on the table.

This East Java Soto *can be considered a complete meal especially when served with a quantity of sliced rice rolls* (Lontong, *page 19*). *Use as much lemon as you like, and refill your bowl periodically with noodles, chicken cubes or anything else that seems tempting. It also makes a festive and practical party dish. Several of the steps can be done in advance, and the* Soto *can easily be integrated into the American kitchen with a minimum of fuss.*

Traditionally a very hot condiment is made from pure, plain steamed hot chili, either fresh or dry. Steam ½ cup chili for ten minutes. Crush the chili in a mortar, and season liberally with lemon juice. This is eaten with the Soto *in direct proportion to your tolerance for the chili.*

¼ teaspoon turmeric
2 cloves garlic, sliced
1 teaspoon chopped fresh ginger
3 kemiri nuts
¼ teaspoon pepper
1 tablespoon peanut or corn oil
One 3-pound chicken, quartered
5 cups of water
2 salam leaves
4 scallions, finely chopped
3 teaspoons salt
2 stalks lemon grass
Two 3-ounce packages cellophane noodles
½ pound bean sprouts
Lemon slices
2 hard-boiled eggs, sliced
Crispy fried onions (see page 224)
Sweet soy sauce (see page 237)

1. Crush together into a paste the turmeric, garlic, ginger, kemiri and pepper. Fry the paste in the oil for one minute.

2. Put the chicken into a pot with the water, salam, two of the scallions, salt, lemon grass and the fried spice paste. Cook covered over medium heat for thirty minutes. Turn off the heat, and let the chicken stand in its broth for fifteen minutes to absorb the flavors. Then remove the meat from the chicken, cut into bite-size pieces and discard the bones.

3. Soak the cellophane noodles in cold water for fifteen minutes, and drain well. Blanch the bean sprouts in hot water for five minutes, and drain well.

4. To serve, prepare separate side dishes of chicken, bean sprouts, the rest of the scallions, cellophane noodles, lemon slices, hot chili, egg slices, crispy onions and sweet soy sauce.

Arrange in layers in the individual soup bowls a tablespoon of chicken, a few bean sprouts, then noodles, scallions, egg, a few drops of sweet soy sauce and hot chili. Add very hot soup and a slice of lemon, and top with the crispy onions. This procedure can be repeated as many times as you wish.
Serves 8

Soto Ayam Madura
CHICKEN SOUP
(MADURA)

10 cloves garlic, sliced
1½ teaspoons pepper
1 tablespoon salt
One 3½-pound chicken, quartered
5½ cups water
1 tablespoon peanut or corn oil
5 fresh green or red hot chilies
½ pound bean sprouts, blanched in hot water for five minutes
One 3-ounce package cellophane noodles, soaked in cold water for fifteen minutes and drained
3 hard-boiled eggs, sliced
Juice of one lemon
1 tablespoon sweet soy sauce *(see page 237)*
4 cups cooked white rice
Potato Fritters, Madura style *(see page 206)*

1. Crush into a paste 6 cloves of the garlic, the pepper and salt. Put the chicken in a large pot with 5 cups of the water,

bring to a boil and add the garlic paste. Fry the 4 remaining garlic cloves in the oil until light brown, and add to the chicken pot. Cook for thirty minutes. The liquid should be reduced to about 4 cups broth.

2. Remove the chicken, and cut the meat into ½-inch cubes, discarding skin and bones. Slice the fresh chilies and cook in the remaining ½ cup water for ten minutes. Drain well, and crush the chilies into a paste. Set aside.

3. In a large serving bowl or tureen, place in layers the bean sprouts, chicken, noodles and egg slices. Add the lemon juice and sweet soy sauce.

4. Heat the broth, and pour it carefully over the ingredients in the bowl. Serve family style in individual bowls. The *Soto* is eaten with cooked white rice, which is added to the bowls as desired. The hot chili is added when needed. The potato fritters are quartered and added to the individual bowls.

Serves 8

❁

Bubur Ayam

CHICKEN AND RICE PORRIDGE

(MENADO, SULAWESI)

The Bubur *probably owes its origins to the Chinese and is reminiscent of* Congee, *a dish in which rice and water are simmered for several hours. The Indonesians have glorified this simple process by creating a luscious dish of chicken, chili, lemon and several other potent flavors combined with the rice porridge. Although this is traditionally a breakfast dish in Indonesia, it would make an ideal party food for the American kitchen. The* Bubur *is popularly known as* Bubur Menado, *revealing the town of its origin.*

- *1 cup rice, washed in cold water several times*
- *5 cups water*
- *1 teaspoon salt*
- *½ 3½-pound chicken*
- *1 teaspoon lemon juice, mixed with ½ teaspoon salt*
- *½ cup peanut or corn oil*
- *1 teaspoon dried hot chili, soaked in 1 tablespoon water*
- *1 tablespoon lemon juice*
- *Crispy fried onions (see page 224)*
- *Crispy fried garlic slices (see page 225)*
- *Bottled fish sauce, Chinese or Thai*
- *½ cup chopped celery leaves*
- *1 fried egg per person (optional)*

1. Simmer the rice, water and salt for about one hour, or until the rice is soft and the mixture thick. This is the basic porridge.

2. Marinate the chicken in the lemon juice and salt mixture for ten minutes. Fry in the oil for ten minutes, or until the chicken is brown. Remove the meat, and cut it into cubes. Discard the bones.

3. Make a condiment by crushing together the chili and 1 tablespoon lemon juice. Fresh red hot chili may be used as well as the dried chili.

4. To serve, put about 1 cup heated rice porridge in a bowl, and sprinkle according to personal taste with chicken, fried onions and garlic, fish sauce, chili and celery leaves. Top with a fried egg if desired.

Serves 4 generously

Laksa

COCONUT MILK IN CHICKEN BROTH WITH GARNISHES

(JAKARTA, JAVA)

Laksa *is a family-style or party soup with a variety of garnishes to be added to the hot broth. Textures and flavors, mix and match, can be varied according to the personal preference of the diner, and those who wish to flex their muscles a bit can indulge in the* Sambal Badjak (*page 243*), *the poor man's volcano.*

- ¼ cup peeled and deveined shrimp
- 2 cloves garlic, sliced
- 1 teaspoon chopped fresh ginger
- ¼ cup sliced onion
- 1 teaspoon coriander
- ¼ teaspoon turmeric
- 2 cups coconut milk (see page 15)
- 2 tablespoons peanut or corn oil
- 2 cups chicken broth
- 1 stalk lemon grass
- 2 teaspoons salt

THE GARNISHES:

- One 2-ounce package cellophane noodles
- 1 cup bean sprouts
- 2 cups cubed cooked chicken
- 2 scallions, chopped

2 hard-boiled eggs, sliced
Crispy fried onion (see page 224)
Sambal Badjak (*see page 243*)

1. Crush the shrimp, garlic, ginger, onion, coriander, turmeric and ½ cup of the coconut milk into a paste in the blender. Heat the oil in a large saucepan, and fry the paste for two minutes.

2. Add the chicken broth, the balance of the coconut milk (1½ cups), the lemon grass and salt, and bring to a boil. Simmer over low heat for five minutes to distribute the flavors.

3. Soak the noodles in hot water for ten minutes; drain and cut in half. Blanch the bean sprouts in hot water for five minutes; drain well.

4. To serve, distribute the garnishes in individual serving bowls, pour ½ cup of the hot broth into each soup plate and add the garnishes to taste.

Serves 6

❁

Soto Babat
SPICED TRIPE SOUP
(SOERABAJA, JAVA)

1½ pounds beef tripe
¼ cup sliced onion
2 cloves garlic, sliced
½ teaspoon black pepper
¼ teaspoon turmeric
1 teaspoon salt
5 cups chicken broth, preferably homemade
1 tablespoon peanut or corn oil
1 piece jeruk purut, or 1 square inch lemon peel (see page 12)
1 slice ginger (1 teaspoon)
2 stalks lemon grass
1 cup boiled chicken, cut into ½-inch cubes

1. Boil the tripe in lightly salted water for about one hour, or until it is soft but still chewy. Discard the liquid, and cut the tripe into ½-inch cubes.

2. In a blender, make a smooth paste of the onion, garlic, pepper, turmeric, salt and ½ cup of the chicken broth. Fry the paste in the oil for two minutes.

3. Add the tripe to the paste, and continue to fry for five minutes more. Add the balance of the broth, the lemon peel, ginger, lemon grass and chicken cubes. Cook slowly for ten minutes to blend flavors. Serve hot.

This soup is usually eaten with plain boiled rice or *Lontong*

(page 19) served separately as a side dish. Some people prefer to add small amounts of rice to the soup while dining.
Serves 8

Sayur Asam Ikan
HOT AND SOUR FISH SOUP
(TUBAN, JAVA)

1½ pounds porgy, sea bass or red snapper
2 cups water
1 clove garlic, sliced thin
¼ cup thin-sliced onion
2 teaspoons tamarind, dissolved in 1 tablespoon water
2 whole green hot chilies
1 teaspoon shrimp (sauce) paste (see page 13)
1 ripe tomato, cubed
2 teaspoons salt
2 teaspoons sugar
1 salam leaf
2 pieces of laos
⅛ teaspoon turmeric

1. Clean the fish, and cut it into six pieces, including the head.

2. Bring the water to a boil in a saucepan, and add all the ingredients except the fish. Boil for five minutes.

3. Add the fish, and cook for fifteen minutes more. The soup is ready and should be eaten hot.
Serves 4

Bayem Cha
SPINACH BROTH
(JAVA)

3 ***cloves garlic, crushed***
1 ***tablespoon peanut or corn oil***
1 ***cup water***
½ ***teaspoon salt***
½ ***teaspoon sugar***
¼ ***teaspoon pepper***
½ ***pound fresh spinach, washed and drained***
1 ***scallion, sliced***

1. Fry the garlic in the oil for a minute in a large saucepan. Add the water, salt, sugar and pepper, and bring to a boil.

2. Add the spinach, and stir for about two minutes, or until the spinach has collapsed. Do not overcook. Serve immediately, garnished with the sliced scallions.

Serves 4, with other dishes

Sayur Bobor
SPINACH AND YELLOW SQUASH SOUP
(MADIUN, EAST JAVA)

This delicious and attractive soup has several faces. It can be served alone, as a straightforward vegetable soup or as one of the dishes in a rijsttafel. *In any event, it is an unusual soup that exemplifies the Indonesian genius for combining vegetables and spices and binding them together with coconut milk.*

1 teaspoon coriander
1 clove garlic sliced
1 slice kencur (¼ teaspoon) (optional)
¼ teaspoon shrimp (sauce) paste (see page 13)
½ cup water
1½ cups coconut milk (see page 15)
1 teaspoon sugar
1 teaspoon salt
1 salam leaf
1 piece of laos
½ pound yellow (summer) squash, cut obliquely into 1-inch triangles
½ pound fresh spinach, washed well and trimmed

1. Crush the coriander, garlic, kencur and shrimp paste in a mortar.

2. Bring the water to a boil in a large saucepan, add the spice paste and cook for one minute. Add 1 cup of the coconut milk, the sugar, salt, salam and laos. Bring to a boil, and add the squash. Stir well, and cook for five minutes. Add the balance of the coconut milk (½ cup) and the spinach; bring to a boil, and serve immediately.

Serves 4 to 6, with other dishes

❂

Sayur Gurih
ZUCCHINI SQUASH SOUP
(JAVA)

- ***1/4 cup thin-sliced fresh semihot chilies***
- ***1/4 cup thin-sliced onion***
- ***1 clove garlic, sliced thin***
- ***2 tablespoons peanut or corn oil***
- ***1 salam leaf***
- ***1 piece of laos***
- ***1/4 cup dried shrimp, cooked in 1/2 cup water for ten minutes***
- ***1/2 teaspoon salt***
- ***1 teaspoon sugar***
- ***1 cup coconut milk*** (*see page 15*)
- ***1 pound zucchini squash, cut into 1-inch cubes***

Fry the chili, onion and garlic in the oil for two minutes. Add the salam and laos. Add the shrimp in its water and all the other ingredients. Cook for about ten minutes, or until the flavors are distributed and the squash has softened. This dish is eaten with *Lontong* (see page 19) or plain rice.

Serves 6, with other dishes

Bihun
FRIED RICE NOODLE MIXTURE
(SUMATRA)

Rice vermicelli are a thin, opaque noodle popular in Southeast Asia that adds a welcome new texture to the American kitchen. A major advantage is that the vermicelli are purchased dry and can remain on the pantry shelf for a substantial length of time. Bihun *is predominantly flavored with two kinds of shrimp, fish balls and crunchy vegetables. Like many dishes from Sumatra, it is just a bit on the acid side, whereas a cook from Java would add sufficient sugar to result in a contrast of flavors.*

Fish balls can be purchased in Chinese or Philippine groceries, either in cans or fresh frozen. The round head or European cabbage, shredded, is an acceptable substitute for the Chinese broccoli.

1 pound dry rice vermicelli
¼ cup sliced onion
5 cloves garlic, sliced thin
2 tablespoons peanut or corn oil
½ pound shrimp, peeled and deveined
¼ cup dried shrimp, soaked in water for thirty minutes and drained
3 tablespoons sweet soy sauce (see page 237)
½ cup thin-sliced celery
½ pound Chinese broccoli, leaves torn into 2-inch pieces and stems discarded
1 cup fish balls, cut in half
¼ cup water
½ teaspoon pepper
¼ cup cubed ripe tomato
1 teaspoon salt

1. Cover the vermicelli with hot water, and soak for thirty minutes. Drain well, and set aside.

2. In a wok or a large frying pan, fry the onion and garlic in the oil until soft and just turning yellow. Add both the fresh and dried shrimp, and stir fry for two minutes. Add the vermicelli, then the sweet soy sauce, celery, broccoli, and fish balls all at once, continuing to stir. Now, add the water, pepper, tomato and, last, the salt, mixing for a minute or two to distribute the ingredients. Total cooking time is about ten minutes. Serve hot or at room temperature.

Serves 6

❁

Bakmi Goreng
FRIED EGG NOODLES
(JAVA)

Fried noodles, with a passing nod to its first cousin, the Chinese lo mein, *is a Javanese national standby. It is an ever-popular concoction that can be assembled in a reasonable time for unexpected guests or as a complete family meal. With a little ingenuity, compatible meat, fish and leafy vegetables can be added or subtracted to the basic recipe, giving the dish a flexibility that precludes endless repetition.*

- 5 *cups water*
- 1 *pound fresh egg noodles*
- 3 *tablespoons peanut or corn oil*
- ¼ *cup thin-sliced onion*
- 2 *cloves garlic, sliced*
- ½ *cup thin-sliced raw boneless chicken*
- ½ *pound shrimp, peeled, deveined and cut into ½-inch pieces*
- 2 *tablespoons soy sauce*
- ½ *cup celery leaves and young stems, cut into ½-inch pieces*
- 3 *scallions, cut into 1-inch pieces*
- 3 *cups bok choy, leaves and young stems cut into 2-inch pieces*
- 1 *teaspoon salt, or to taste*
- ¼ *teaspoon pepper*

1. Bring the water to a boil in a large saucepan, and add the noodles. Cook for three minutes, stirring occasionally. Drain immediately, and rinse under cold water. Mix the noodles with 1 tablespoon of the oil, and set aside.

2. Crush 2 tablespoons of the onion and the garlic into a paste. Fry in the remaining 2 tablespoons oil in a wok for a minute, adding the remaining onions. Add the chicken and shrimp, and fry for two minutes. Now add the soy sauce, celery, scallions, bok choy, salt and pepper, and fry for about two minutes. Add the noodles, and mix well for two minutes so that all the ingredients will be evenly distributed. Serve hot or at room temperature.

Variation: One or two cups of watercress can be used to supplement the celery leaves and stems. The watercress, with its slightly bitter flavor, adds an irrestible contrast with the soft fried noodles.

Serves 6, with other dishes

Mostly Chicken

Chicken may well be the most popular meat in the Indonesian archipelago, and the variety of ways to cook this ubiquitous farmyard bird are apparently endless. Most of the dishes can be described as a form of stew, generally lubricated with quantities of coconut milk and flavored with the standard spices in the Indonesian repertory. The other basic method of preparing chicken, depending on the island preference, could be construed as dry, that is, barbecued or with most, if not all, of the sauce allowed to evaporate in cooking. Fried chicken (*Ayam Goreng*), dishes would come under this category. My Sumatran friends prefer their fried chicken to be crisp and chewy, whereas we might consider this overdone. However, becoming acquainted with unfamiliar textures from another culture helps us expand our culinary horizons and explains the enormous variety found in Indonesian cooking.

delicious!

Opor Ayam

BRAISED CHICKEN IN COCONUT MILK

(JAVA)

This is a classic Indonesian recipe, encompassing all the unconventional flavors and spices of the archipelago, generously laced together with coconut milk. It is, in effect, a library of flavors blended together in what could be described as the Indonesian taste. No knowledge of Indonesian cooking is complete without Opor Ayam, *nor should any large* rijsttafel, *in my opinion, do without it. The dish may be cooked in advance and refrigerated for up to two days, or it may be frozen until needed. Thaw at room temperature for two hours before reheating.*

1 3½-pound chicken
1 tablespoon lemon juice
¼ cup thin-sliced onion
1 clove garlic, sliced thin
⅛ teaspoon turmeric
1 teaspoon coriander
¼ teaspoon ground cumin
2 kemiri nuts, crushed
1 slice ginger—about 1 teaspoon
¼ teaspoon pepper
2 cups coconut milk (see page 15)
1 tablespoon peanut or corn oil
1 teaspoon tamarind, dissolved in 1 tablespoon water

1 teaspoon salt
1 teaspoon sugar
2 salam leaves
1 piece of laos
1 piece of jeruk purut, or 1 square inch of lemon peel (see page 12)

1. Cut the chicken into eight pieces, discard the loose skin and fat and rub the pieces with the lemon juice. Broil for five minutes, turn the pieces over and broil for five minutes more. The chicken will be partially cooked and firm.

2. In a blender, prepare a smooth sauce of the onion, garlic, turmeric, coriander, cumin, kemiri nuts, ginger, pepper and ½ cup of the coconut milk.

3. Heat the oil in a saucepan or wok, and add the sauce. Fry for two minutes; then add the balance of the coconut milk, the tamarind liquid, salt, sugar, salam, laos and jeruk purut. Add the pieces of precooked chicken, and bring to a boil over medium heat. Cook for five minutes, basting frequently; then continue to cook for twenty minutes more. The liquid will have reduced to a rather thick sauce, and the chicken will be tender but still firm.

Serves 6, with other dishes

❂

Ayam Bumbu Rujak
MIXED SPICE CHICKEN
(SOERABAJA, JAVA)

This dish will keep for up to two days in the refrigerator, or it may be made in advance and frozen. Thaw for two hours at room temperature before reheating.

- *¼ cup sliced onion*
- *3 cloves garlic, sliced*
- *2 teaspoons crushed dried red hot chili*
- *5 kemiri nuts, crushed*
- *⅛ teaspoon turmeric*
- *1 teaspoon salt*
- *1 teaspoon sugar*
- *2 cups coconut milk (see page 15)*
- *1 tablespoon peanut or corn oil*
- *One 3½-pound chicken, cut into frying pieces*
- *1 thick slice ginger*
- *1 stalk lemon grass*

1. Blend the onion, garlic, chili, kemiri, turmeric, salt and sugar with ¼ cup of the coconut milk into a paste. Fry in the oil for one minute.

2. Add the chicken, ginger, and lemon grass, and fry for five minutes more over medium heat. Then add the balance of the coconut milk (1¾ cups), and cook for forty-five minutes, basting

frequently. The sauce will have thickened and evaporated somewhat, and the chicken will be tender.
Serves 6, with other dishes

❁

Ayam Kodok
STUFFED CHICKEN IN THE SHAPE OF A FROG
(JAVA)

This extraordinary dish is of European, probably Dutch origin, but it has assumed Indonesian characteristics. It is a boneless stuffed chicken that acquires the flattened shape of a frog after being stuffed. Steamed and then roasted, the twice-cooked chicken introduces a new cooking technique into the American kitchen that produces a culinary triumph. Mastering this recipe not only will enhance the prestige of the cook but will produce a useful and luscious buffet item for the rijsttafel. *In Indonesia the neck and head of the chicken are still attached to the skin, a more realistic touch which makes for a somewhat macabre apparition. However, this step will not be included for our purposes.*

One 3½ to 4-pound chicken
1 cup carrots, diced in ¼ inch cubes
¼ cup chopped onion
2 cloves garlic, chopped
2 tablespoons butter
2 raw eggs, beaten
1 teaspoon salt
½ teaspoon pepper
½ teaspoon nutmeg
½ cup fresh or frozen green peas
3 slices white bread, cubed, soaked in water for two minutes and squeezed dry
4 hard-boiled eggs, shelled

Aluminum foil

1. Skin the chicken as directed below. Remove the meat from the sections of breast, thighs and legs. Discard bits of skin and tendons, and cut the meat into small cubes. This should produce about 3 cups. The carcass can be used to make stock for other recipes.

2. Drop the carrots in boiling water for one minute, and drain well. Set aside. Fry the onion and garlic in the butter for about two minutes, or until soft and golden. Allow this mixture to cool.

3. Pulverize the chicken meat in a blender or food processor. Mix the paste with the raw eggs, salt, pepper, nutmeg, fried onion/garlic, the peas, carrots and bread. Stir into a fairly smooth mixture.

4. Spread out the chicken skin, and put half the stuffing in the center of the more or less rectangular shape. Place 2 of the hard-boiled eggs near the neck end and 2 near each of the legs. Cover the eggs with the balance of the stuffing. Sew up the

chicken, starting with the neck and wings and continuing to the tail end. Press the stuffing gently into the hollow legs, and distribute it evenly throughout the bird. Should parts of the skin be torn they can be repaired in the sewing process.

5. Rest the chicken on a square of aluminum foil, and shape it into a slightly flattened object, the legs crossed in back, froglike, and the wings resting on top. Place the chicken and foil in a Chinese-style steamer, and steam over medium/high heat for thirty minutes.

Note: At this stage, the steamed chicken can be frozen for future use or refrigerated for *one* day before proceeding to the next step in the preparation. Allow the steamed chicken to cool for thirty minutes, and wrap it completely first in aluminum foil, then in a plastic bag. Store in the freezer for as long as necessary. Having completed the *Ayam Kodok* to this stage will be of enormous advantage when one is considering the preparation of ten to fifteen dishes. Before proceeding to the roasting step, it is essential that the chicken be removed from the freezer and defrosted for about four hours at room temperature, or overnight in the refrigerator.

6. Put the chicken in a well-oiled roasting pan, and bake in a 400-degree oven for thirty minutes, or until the skin has turned a crispy brown.

7. To serve, pull out the sewing thread, and cut the chicken in half vertically down the center. Cut generous slices horizontally from the two halves. The chicken is traditionally served with a variety of plain cooked vegetables, such as carrots, peas, string beans, cabbage and potatoes, both boiled and fried.

How to Skin the Chicken

1. With the reverse (blunt) edge of a cleaver, break the legs of the chicken 1 inch from the bottom of the ankle. This is done by giving the leg a sharp whack which will break off an inch of bone without tearing the skin.

2. From the neck end of the chicken, loosen the skin all around the joints of the wings with your fingers. Cut through the joint and meat without cutting the skin and, pulling with your fingers, detach the wings from the body, leaving them attached to the skin.

3. With the chicken turned breast side up, cut through the skin in one long incision from the neck end to the bottom, and with your fingers loosen the skin along the breast from the body. Pull out the legs which have been broken off. This should loosen all the skin from the breast side.

4. The back is firmly attached to the skin. Cut it carefully from the body with a sharp knife. The tail should be included with the skin which is now loosened from the carcass and can be opened out into a more or less rectagular shape, including the two wings, the tail and the ends of the legs. The skin is now ready to be stuffed and reshaped into a froglike animal.

Serves 10, with other dishes

❂

Ayam Goreng
FRIED CHICKEN JAKARTA
(JAVA)

This method of frying chicken is a specialty of Jakarta, the capital of Indonesia on the island of Java. The pieces are first cooked in a heavily spiced sauce which permeates the chicken and then fried in hot oil to brown. It is a popular picnic dish which can be eaten hot or cold and tastes better the second day when I have broiled it for three minutes to reheat. The sauce that remains after the chicken is cooked is fine for seasoning plain white rice. An economical and exotic dish without waste.

One 3½-pound chicken, cut into frying pieces
- **3 *teaspoons salt***
- **2 *teaspoons lemon juice***
- **¼ *cup sliced onion***
- **3 *kemiri nuts, crushed***
- **1 *fresh red hot chili, sliced***
- **2 *teaspoons coriander***
- **¼ *teaspoon turmeric***
- **½ *cup water***
- **1 *tablespoon tamarind, dissolved in 2 tablespoons water***
- **1 *piece of laos***
- **1 *stalk lemon grass***
- **½ *cup peanut or corn oil***

1. Rub the chicken with 1 teaspoon of the salt and the lemon juice. Let it stand for ten minutes; then rinse under cold water. Drain well.

2. In the blender, make a sauce of the onion, kemiri, the remaining 2 teaspoons salt, the chili, coriander, turmeric and water. Pour this over the chicken pieces in a saucepan, and add the tamarind liquid, laos and lemon grass. Cook over medium heat for twenty minutes, or until most of the liquid has evaporated. Remove the chicken, and fry it in medium/hot oil for about five

minutes, or until it turns crispy brown. Remove, and drain on paper towels.
Serves 6, with other dishes

Ayam Goreng
FRIED CHICKEN, INDONESIAN STYLE
(CENTRAL JAVA)

1 clove garlic, crushed
1 teaspoon salt
1 teaspoon tamarind, dissolved in 1 tablespoon water
One 3½-pound broiler, cut up for frying into about 10 pieces
½ cup peanut or corn oil

1. Mix the garlic, salt and tamarind liquid into a sauce, and marinate the chicken pieces in this mixture for fifteen minutes.
2. Heat the oil in a wok or frying pan, and fry the pieces of chicken for about fifteen minutes, or until they are brown and crispy. Drain well on paper towels. This may be eaten hot or at room temperature.

Serves 4, with other dishes

Gulai Wellie
CHICKEN MAKASSAR SAUTÉ
(SULAWESI)

I have seen an Indonesian woman reduce freshly-grated coconut meat to a brown, rich, thick paste like molten lava in a large, family-size stone mortar and pestle. From one corner of the mortar to another, with coconut milk added to lubricate the process, the twisting wrist movements against the mortar became a rhythmic routine. It was an extraordinary primitive but effective demonstration of village culinary activity. Now we use a blender or food processor, but it does not seem the same.

One 3½-pound chicken, cut into frying pieces
1 cup grated coconut
2 cups coconut milk (see page 15)
2 teaspoons tamarind, dissolved in 1 tablespoon water
1 teaspoon salt
¼ cup sliced onion
3 cloves garlic, sliced
2 stalks lemon grass

1. Broil the chicken pieces on both sides for about ten minutes, or until they are brown.

2. Toast the coconut in a dry frying pan, turning frequently over a low flame, until it is light brown. Put it through the blender with the coconut milk to prepare a thick, smooth paste.

3. Put the chicken, coconut paste, tamarind liquid, salt, onion, garlic and lemon grass in a saucepan, and cook for about thirty minutes, or until nearly all the liquid has evaporated and the chicken is tender.
Serves 6, with other dishes

۞

Magadip
AROMATIC CHICKEN
(MADURA)

The Magadip *has proved to be one of the most popular Indonesian chicken recipes in my repertoire. Toasting the dry spices for several minutes releases the essential oils and imparts a mouth-watering aromatic flavor to the chicken. The recipe does not require garlic, hot chili or coconut milk, in itself making this an unconventional chicken dish in the Indonesian galaxy. As an additional attraction, it can be made in advance and kept in the refrigerator for up to two days, or frozen until needed. Thaw at room temperature for two hours before reheating.*

¼ cup thin-sliced onion
2 teaspoons salt
1 cup water
1 tablespoon coriander
1 teaspoon pepper
1 teaspoon ground cumin
¼ teaspoon ground clove
¼ teaspoon nutmeg
One 2-inch cinnamon stick

¼ teaspoon turmeric
1 slice ginger (about 1 teaspoon)
One 3½-pound chicken, cut into frying pieces

1. In a blender, make a smooth sauce of the onion, salt and ½ cup of water.

2. Mix the coriander, pepper, cumin, clove, nutmeg, cinnamon and turmeric together in a dry saucepan. Toast lightly over medium heat for about two minutes. Add the onion sauce and the balance of the water (½ cup) to the saucepan, along with the ginger and the chicken pieces. Cook over medium heat for about forty-five minutes, or until the chicken is tender and about half the sauce has evaporated.

Variation: The *Magadip* can be made with 2 pounds boneless lamb, cut into 2-inch cubes, as a substitute for the chicken. The total cooking time should be extended to about one hour fifteen minutes, or until the lamb is tender. Should the liquid evaporate too quickly, ½ cup water can be added.
Serves 6, with other dishes

Ayam Blado
BROWNED CHICKEN IN HOT SAUCE
(SUMATRA)

The Blado *has several of the characteristics of Sumatran cooking, including a tolerance for hot chili and an unconventional texture to the well-done, slightly dry chicken pieces. The combination is most interesting, and this dish incorporates well into a* rijsttafel.

½ cup water
½ cup sliced onion
6 cloves garlic, sliced
1 tablespoon salt
Two 3-pound chickens, cut into frying pieces, loose skin and fat discarded
½ cup peanut or corn oil
3 tablespoons fresh red hot chili, blended into a paste
1 cup chicken stock

1. In the blender, make a sauce of the water, ¼ cup of the onion, 3 cloves of the garlic and the salt. Cook the chicken in this sauce for twenty minutes; remove it, and reserve the spiced sauce, which should measure about 1 cup.

2. Brown the chicken well in half the oil over medium heat for about ten minutes. Remove, and set aside. Fry the remainder of the onion and garlic in the remaining oil until it is light brown; then add the chili, reserved sauce and stock, and cook for five minutes, or until the sauce is reduced by about one-half. Add the chicken, and baste well to coat with the sauce. Serve hot or at room temperature.

Serves 8, with other dishes

Masak Hidjau

GREEN CHICKEN

(BORNEO-KALIMANTAN)

We are told the name Green Chicken comes from the green, crunchy slices of sweet pepper in this recipe.

One 3½-pound chicken, cut into frying pieces
10 tablespoons peanut or corn oil
1 cup water
¼ cup sliced onion
1 teaspoon dried red hot chili
1 slice ginger (1 teaspoon)
1 slice kencur (¼ teaspoon), soaked in water for fifteen minutes (optional)
¼ teaspoon shrimp (sauce) paste (*see page 13*)
1 teaspoon salt
½ teaspoon turmeric
2 salam leaves
2 pieces of laos
1 stalk lemon grass
1 ripe tomato, cubed
1 large green sweet pepper, cut into ½-inch-wide slices

1. Fry the pieces of chicken in ½ cup of the oil for about ten minutes, or until they are well browned. Remove, and set aside.

2. In the blender, prepare a sauce of the water, onion, garlic, chili, ginger, kencur, shrimp paste, salt and turmeric. Fry the sauce in the remaining 2 tablespoons oil for five minutes. Add the chicken, salam, laos and lemon grass, and stir well.

3. Cook the mixture over medium heat for fifteen minutes, or until the flavors are distributed and the sauce has been reduced by half. Then add the tomato and green pepper, and cook for two minutes longer.

Serves 6, with other dishes

❁

Gulai Ayam
SUMATRA SPICED CHICKEN

The Gulai *of Sumatra is said to be of Arab origin and is a typical Sumatran dish. Originally a whole lamb was used, the tender portions for* satay *and the balance of the meat in the* Gulai. *It is one of the foods prepared ceremonially for Ramadan, the Islamic New Year.*

3 kemiri nuts, crushed
3 cloves garlic, sliced
¼ cup sliced onion
1 teaspoon dried red hot chili, soaked in 2 teaspoons water
2 cups coconut milk (see page 15)
2 tablespoons peanut or corn oil
One 3½-pound chicken, cut into frying pieces
2 teaspoons coriander
¼ teaspoon turmeric
2 teaspoons salt
2 teaspoons light or dark brown sugar
2 salam leaves
1 piece of laos

1. In the blender, prepare a paste of the kemiri, garlic, onion, chili and ¼ cup of the coconut milk.

2. Fry the paste in the oil for one minute, and add the chicken, the balance of the coconut milk, the coriander, turmeric, salt, sugar, salam and laos. Cook over medium flame,

basting frequently, for about forty-five minutes, or until the chicken is soft and the sauce has been reduced by half.
Serves 6, with other dishes

❂

Nasi Tim
CHICKEN IN RICE
(WEST JAVA)

¼ cup sliced onion
3 cloves garlic, sliced
1½ cups coconut milk (see page 15)
One 3½-pound chicken, cut into frying pieces
1 teaspoon salt
1 teaspoon sugar
2 salam leaf
1 piece of laos
¼ teaspoon pepper
¼ teaspoon ground cumin
2 teaspoons coriander
3 pieces of jeruk purut, or 3 square inches of lemon peel (see page 12)
2 cups rice
3½ cups water

Aluminum foil

1. In a blender, make a sauce of the onion, garlic and ½ cup of the coconut milk.
2. Put the chicken in a saucepan, and pour the sauce over it.

Add the salt, sugar, salam, laos, pepper, cumin, coriander, jeruk purut and the remaining 1 cup coconut milk. Cook for twenty-five to thirty minutes, or until almost all the sauce has evaporated and the chicken is soft.

3. Cook the rice and water together in another pan, covered, for ten minutes. Turn off the heat, and allow the pan to stand for ten more minutes, covered.

4. Line a Chinese-style steamer with a large square of aluminum foil. Add a layer of rice about 1 inch thick, then add several pieces of chicken and 1 tablespoon sauce. Repeat until all the rice and chicken are used, with the rice on top as the final layer. Cover the steamer, and cook over medium/high heat for twenty minutes. To serve, unfold the chicken and rice onto a platter in a rounded mound, covering the chicken pieces with the rice.

Variation: Layer the chicken and rice in a glass fireproof casserole (Pyrex) that will fit into a steamer and then go directly to the table.
Serves 6, with other dishes

Kalio

CHICKEN IN COCONUT MILK

(SUMATRA)

Kalio *is another variation on the chicken bathed in a coconut milk sauce. Characteristically the predominant flavors of lemon grass, tomato, ginger and hot chili inform us of its Sumatran origins.*

Two 3-pound chickens
5 cloves garlic, sliced
½ cup thin-sliced onion
½ teaspoon turmeric
One 1-inch piece ginger, sliced thin
¼ cup chopped tomato
2 teaspoons salt
3 tablespoons crushed fresh red hot chili
2½ cups coconut milk (see page 15)
1 stalk lemon grass
2 salam leaf
1 piece of laos
2 tablespoons peanut or corn oil

1. Cut the chicken into frying pieces, discarding the loose skin and fat.

2. Fry the garlic and onion in the oil for two minutes, or until light brown. Add the turmeric, ginger, tomato, salt and chili. Stir well, and fry for two minutes more.

3. Add the chicken, and fry for three minutes. Then add the coconut milk, lemon grass, salam and laos, and cook for forty-five minutes over medium heat, basting frequently. When done, the sauce should be reduced by half, and the chicken tender.

Serves 8, with other dishes

❁

Ayam Panggang Klaten
CHICKEN IN AROMATIC NUT SAUCE
(KLATEN, CENTRAL JAVA)

A richly thick nut sauce composed of tastily seasoned coconut milk reduced to a creamy consistency is the outstanding characteristic of this crisp grilled Java chicken.

10 kemiri nuts, crushed
¼ cup thin-sliced onion
3 cloves garlic, sliced
½ teaspoon ground cumin
2 teaspoons coriander
2 teaspoons sugar
1 teaspoon salt
¼ teaspoon shrimp (sauce) paste (see page 13)
2½ cups coconut milk (see page 15)
One 3½-pound chicken, split open and flattened out
5 pieces of jeruk purut, or 5 square inches of lemon peel (see page 12)
3 salam leaves
3 pieces of laos

1. Blend the kemiri, onion, garlic, cumin, coriander, sugar, salt, shrimp paste and ½ cup of the coconut milk to a smooth paste.
2. Broil the chicken for five minutes on each side.

3. Put the spice paste in a wok or large frying pan, and add the balance of the coconut milk, the jeruk purut, salam and laos. Bring to a boil, add the chicken and cook in the sauce for twenty minutes, basting frequently. When done, the sauce will have almost completely evaporated.

4. Return the chicken, skin side up, and the balance of the sauce to the broiler and broil for ten minutes, or until the chicken is brown and crispy. Serve hot.

Serves 6, with other dishes

Kare Ayam
CHICKEN CURRY, JAVA STYLE

Java curry is moderately flavored, scented with lemon grass, jeruk purut and the salam leaves of Java, combined with the curry powder which leads it directly to the Indian connection. But included with the chicken are three vegetables which complete the conversion to the Indonesian way of life. I have found this curry to be extremely popular among my guests. Rice, one of the island salads and krupuk *(page 203) complete the ethnic balance of the meal. With, of course, as much chili as you can tolerate served separately as a condiment.*

¼ cup sliced onion
2 cloves garlic, sliced
1 tablespoon peanut or corn oil
1 tablespoon curry powder
One 3½-pound chicken, cut into frying pieces
½ cup water
2 teaspoons salt
2 teaspoons sugar
3 pieces of jeruk purut, or 3 square inches of lemon peel (see page 12)
2 salam leaves
1 stalk lemon grass
½ cup potato, cut into ½-inch cubes
⅓ cup carrots, sliced julienne
½ cup string beans, cut into 2-inch pieces
1½ cups coconut milk (see page 15)
One 3-ounce package cellophane noodles (optional)

Fry the onion and garlic in the oil for two minutes. Add the curry powder, and stir well; then add the chicken pieces, and brown slightly. Add the water and, when boiling, the salt, sugar, jeruk purut, salam, lemon grass, potatoes, carrots, and string beans. Stir well. Finally, add the coconut milk, and baste frequently so that the milk does not curdle and the sauce evolves smoothly. Cook the curry over medium heat for thirty minutes, then add the cellophane noodles if desired. Cook ten minutes more, or until the chicken is soft. This curry does have ample sauce.

Serves 6

❂

Ayam Lapis
CHICKEN LEAVES
(JAVA)

The name Chicken Leaves is descriptive of the chicken slices, which are reminiscent of the small, thin leaves of a tree.

1 *boneless breast of chicken, cut into thin slices*
2 *tablespoons chopped onion*
¼ *teaspoon pepper*
¼ *teaspoon nutmeg*
⅛ *teaspoon ground clove*
½ *teaspoon salt*
1 *tablespoon sweet soy sauce (see page 237)*
1 *teaspoon tomato ketchup*
1 *egg, beaten*
1 *tablespoon butter*
½ *cup water*

1. Add the chicken, onion, pepper, nutmeg, clove, salt, sweet soy sauce and tomato ketchup to the beaten egg. Mix well.

2. Melt the butter in a frying pan, and over medium heat, add the chicken mixture. Fry for three minutes, add the water and cook for ten minutes more. When done, the sauce will have thickened and the flavors will have been distributed. The *Lapis* is eaten with an assortment of boiled vegetables, such as carrots, green peas, sliced potatoes and string beans. Serve hot or at room temperature.

Serves 4, with other dishes

Ayam Panggang Pecel
BROILED CHICKEN IN RAW COCONUT MILK
(JAVA)

I first tasted this oddly flavored, uncooked coconut sauce as one of the ceremonial dishes made to celebrate a business anniversary. According to Indonesian custom, it was served among many dishes at room temperature on a hot day, a very appropriate combination.

One 3½-pound chicken
1½ cups coconut milk (see page 15)
2 cloves garlic
1 teaspoon dried red hot chili, soaked in 1 tablespoon water for half an hour
½ teaspoon shrimp (sauce) paste (see page 13)
1 teaspoon salt
2 teaspoons sugar
1 teaspoon tamarind, dissolved in 2 teaspoons water
1 slice kencur (¼ teaspoon), soaked in 1 tablespoon water for half an hour (optional)

1. Split the chicken open through the breast and flatten it out. Broil the chicken for ten minutes or a bit more on each side, or until it is cooked through. Cut several strokes through the chicken to provide an entry for the sauce.

2. In a blender, make a sauce of ½ cup of the coconut milk, the garlic, chili, shrimp paste, salt, sugar, tamarind liquid and kencur in its liquid, if desired. Mix this with the balance of the coconut milk (1 cup), and pour over the broiled chicken.
Serves 6, with other dishes

❁

Ajam Ingkung
WHITE FEATHER CEREMONIAL ROOSTER
(JAVA)

1 whole 4-pound chicken or capon
4 cups coconut milk (see page 15)
3 cloves garlic, sliced
¼ cup sliced onion
7 kemiri nuts, crushed
½ teaspoon ground cumin
1 tablespoon coriander
1 teaspoon pepper
¼ teaspoon turmeric
¼ teaspoon shrimp (sauce) paste (see page 13)
1 teaspoon sugar
2 teaspoons salt
3 salam leaves
2 pieces of laos

1. Ceremonially speaking, the chicken or capon should have both head and feet still on during the cooking process. Using wooden cocktail skewers, fix the wings along the sides of the

bird, and keep head and neck upright in a sitting position. Place the chicken in a large saucepan.

2. In the blender, make a sauce of ½ cup of the coconut milk, the garlic, onion, kemiri, cumin, coriander, pepper, turmeric, shrimp paste, sugar and salt. Pour the sauce over the chicken, add the balance of the coconut milk (3½ cups), the salam and laos.

3. Bring to a boil, and baste the chicken continuously for about fifteen minutes. Cover the pan, and cook over medium heat for thirty minutes more, basting occasionally. The chicken should maintain its sitting position throughout the cooking. When done, the sauce will have reduced by about 1 cup.

4. Transfer the chicken to a platter. Remove the skewers, and pour the sauce over it. Serve at room temperature.

The same recipe may be used without the ceremonial activities of head, feet and skewers. It becomes a tender, tasty, spicy chicken or capon with the classic and traditional flavors of Indonesian food.

Serves 8, with other dishes

Ayam Panggang Kecap
BARBECUED CHICKEN IN SWEET SOY SAUCE
(TUBAN, JAVA)

Sweet soy sauce, reconstituted from a dark Chinese soy sauce with caramelized sugar and various spices added, must be considered the most popular and universally accepted of Indonesian flavorings. It lends excitement to any food. This barbecued chicken is deservedly popular, easy to prepare and easier to eat. It can be eaten hot, cold or at room temperature, but Americans may well prefer it hot. I urge you to try it.

One 3½-pound chicken, split in half along the breast side and opened flat
3 cloves garlic, sliced thin
2 fresh semihot chilies, sliced thin
1 tablespoon peanut or corn oil
1 teaspoon tamarind, dissolved in 2 teaspoons water
¼ cup water
1 teaspoon sugar
5 tablespoons sweet soy sauce (see page 237)
1 slice fresh ginger (1 teaspoon)

1. Broil the chicken for five minutes on each side.

2. Fry the garlic and chilies in the oil for one minute in a large frying pan. Add the tamarind liquid, water, sugar, sweet soy sauce and ginger, and cook over low heat for about five minutes, or until the sauce has thickened. Set aside.

3. Remove the chicken from the broiler, and pound it lightly all over with a pestle to bruise the meat and allow the sauce to seep in. Put the chicken, skin side down, in the frying pan with the sauce, and cook over medium heat for about ten minutes, or until nearly all the sauce has evaporated.

4. Return the chicken, skin side up, to the broiler and broil for five minutes, or until the skin is brown and crispy.

Serves 4 to 6, with other dishes

Ayam Panggang Setan

RED DEVIL BARBECUED CHICKEN

(SOLO, JAVA)

This chili-hot chicken, the hotter the better, is a specialty of the city of Solo in Central Java. The barbecue is served hot or at room temperature—remember that room temperature on a summer day in Java could be 100 degrees or more. It is also a popular picnic dish. Cut the chicken into pieces after broiling, and serve it with cold rice packed into banana leaves.

One 3½-pound broiler, split open along the breast side and opened flat
2 fresh red or green hot chilies, sliced thin
3 cloves garlic, sliced thin
¼ cup thin sliced onion
¼ teaspoon shrimp (sauce) paste (see page 13)
1 teaspoon salt
2 teaspoons sugar
1 tablespoon tamarind, dissolved in 2 tablespoons water
1½ cups coconut milk (see page 15)

1. Broil the chicken for ten minutes on each side.

2. In the blender, make a fairly smooth sauce of the chilies, garlic, onion, shrimp paste, salt, sugar, tamarind liquid and coconut milk. Cook the sauce in a large frying pan for five minutes to distribute the flavors.

3. Remove the chicken from the broiler, and pound it all over lightly with a pestle to bruise the meat so that the sauce can penetrate. Put the chicken in the frying pan with the sauce, and fry it over medium heat, basting frequently, for ten minutes, or until most of the liquid has evaporated. Then return the chicken to the broiler, skin side up, pour on the sauce and broil for five minutes, or until it is crisp and sizzling.
Serves 4 to 6, with other dishes

❁

Asam Asam

STEAMED PUNGENT CHICKEN GIBLETS

(SOERABAJA, JAVA)

The women of Soerabaja, a large seaport in East Java, who are celebrated for their cooking, seem to have a particular liking for salty food. The mothers enjoy the traditions associated with the home and domestic life in general and impart a sense of discipline to their daughters. The Asam Asam *is an easy dish to assemble, with a variety of textures and flavors. Like any casserole, it is a welcome adjunct to an Indonesian meal.*

½ pound chicken gizzards
½ pound chicken livers
¼ pound chicken hearts
¼ cup thin-sliced onion
4 cloves garlic, sliced
1½ cups coconut milk (see page 15)
¼ teaspoon shrimp (sauce) paste (see page 13)
2 fresh green semihot chilies, sliced thin

- *2 teaspoons tamarind, dissolved in 1 tablespoon water*
- *1 teaspoon salt*
- *1 teaspoon sugar*
- *1 ripe tomato, cubed*
- *½ cup fresh or canned mushrooms (optional)*
- *1 salam leaf*
- *1 piece of laos*

1. Trim the cartilage from the gizzards, and score them in three places. Cut the livers into lobes. Split the hearts open.

2. In the blender, make a paste of the onion, garlic and ½ cup of the coconut milk. Add the paste and all other ingredients, including the balance of the coconut milk, to a fireproof (Pyrex) dish. Mix well, and steam in a Chinese-style steamer over medium heat for one hour.

Serves 8, with other dishes

❁

Sambal Goreng Ati

CHICKEN LIVERS SAUTÉ WITH SNOW PEAS

(JAVA)

¼ pound fresh snow peas
1 pound chicken livers
2 cups water
¼ cup thin-sliced onion
2 cloves garlic, sliced thin
1 tablespoon peanut or corn oil
½ red sweet pepper, sliced thin
1 cup coconut milk (see page 15)
1 teaspoon salt
1 teaspoon sugar
¼ teaspoon shrimp (sauce) paste (see page 13)
2 salam leaf
1 piece of laos
1 teaspoon tamarind, dissolved in 1 tablespoon water
1 teaspoon dried red hot chili

1. String the snow peas, and refrigerate them in cold water for thirty minutes before using. Drain well.

2. Boil the livers in water for two minutes. Drain well, and cut in lobes.

3. Fry the onion and garlic in the oil for one minute, add the sweet pepper and fry for another minute. Add the coconut milk, salt, sugar, shrimp paste, salam, laos, tamarind liquid, chili

and the livers. Cook for about five minutes, basting frequently to distribute the flavors. Add the snow peas, and cook for two minutes more. Do not overcook so that the snow peas will provide a contrasting texture to the liver.

Variation: Beef liver may be used to good advantage instead of the chicken livers. The same system of preparation is used except the beef liver is cubed before being boiled. The result is a combination that has more texture and a darker flavor.

Sambal Goreng Ati

SWEET, HOT LIVERS SAUTÉ

(JAVA)

1 pound chicken livers
1 cup water
3 tablespoons peanut or corn oil
¼ cup sliced onion
1 clove garlic, sliced
1 tablespoon fresh hot red chili, sliced thin diagonally
¼ cup thin-sliced red sweet pepper
1 teaspoon tamarind, dissolved in 1 tablespoon water
1 teaspoon salt
1 tablespoon sugar
1 salam leaf
1 piece of laos

1. Divide the livers in lobes, and boil in the water for five minutes. Discard the water.

2. Fry the livers in the medium/hot oil for about two minutes, or until they are light brown. Set aside. Fry the onion, garlic, hot chili and sweet pepper in the same oil. Add the tamarind liquid, salt, sugar, salam and laos, and fry for two minutes longer. Add the livers, and fry for two minutes more to distribute the flavors.

Variation: Substitute beef liver, cut into ½-inch cubes. Boil in 1 cup water, as for the chicken livers, and continue according to the directions above. Beef liver has a chewier texture than chicken livers. Combined with this sweet and sour sauce, it is an altogether delicious method of cooking one of the internal organs that is not always everyone's cup of tea.
Serves 6, with other dishes

Bebek Bumbu Bali
BALINESE DUCK
(BALI)

The island of Bali is a Hindu isle in a sea of Islam. The religion of Bali is derived directly from the early Hindu and Buddhist wayfarers from India, who transmitted their culture to the Indonesian archipelago in about the fifth century A.D.

The Balinese today have retained the gods of the Hindus and have integrated them with the characteristics of their pre-Hindu nature gods. Animism is the worship of the cosmos as it manifests itself in nature. In Balinese family shrines, daily of-

ferings of food, flowers and fruit are offered to placate the evil spirits in the ever-constant battle between good and evil.

This braised Bebek *in nut sauce is a delicious rarity. I have always prepared it one day in advance and refrigerated it so that the considerable congealed fat that accumulates can be more easily discarded. Or it can be made well in advance and frozen. American ducks are fat, and a substantial amount of fat and skin should be removed before cooking. The dish is then an admirable adjunct to any Indonesian dinner. It should be served with several cooked vegetable dishes reflecting the cuisines of several different islands, plus rice and a salad.*

One 4½- to 5-pound duck
10 kemiri nuts, crushed
½ teaspoon shrimp (sauce) paste (see page 13)
1 tablespoon dried red hot chili, soaked in 2 tablespoons water
¼ cup sliced onion
5 cloves garlic, sliced
2 tablespoons sweet soy sauce (see page 237)
½ teaspoon turmeric
2 teaspoons salt
2 cups water
4 salam leaves
2 pieces of laos
2 stalks lemon grass

1. Disjoint the duck, and cut it into about 10 pieces. Trim and discard the loose skin and fat.

2. In the blender, prepare a sauce of the kemiri, shrimp paste, chili, onion, garlic, sweet soy sauce, turmeric, salt and ½

cup of the water. Cook the sauce for three minutes in a large saucepan that will accommodate the duck.

3. Add the duck, salam, laos, lemon grass and the balance of the water (1½ cups). Stir well, and cook over medium heat for about one and a half hours, or until the duck is soft and about half the sauce has evaporated. Should the duck appear to be too dry, ½ cup water can be added during the cooking process.
Serves 6, with other dishes

Opor Bebek
BRAISED, STUFFED DUCK IN NUT SAUCE
(SEMARANG, CENTRAL JAVA)

Indonesians are not by nature terribly fond of ducks, which are raised more for their eggs than the meat. They consider ducks a preoccupation of the Chinese. Be that as it may, this recipe was given to me by an Indonesian friend who described it as an old family recipe. The ingredients and flavors are quintessentially Indonesian, but the oven roasting smacks very much of a Dutch colonial hand.

- *4 cups coconut milk (see page 15)*
- *¼ cup sliced onion*
- *3 cloves garlic, sliced*
- *1 tablespoon tamarind, soaked in 2 tablespoons water*
- *2 teaspoons sliced fresh red or green hot chili*
- *1 teaspoon ground cumin*
- *1 tablespoon coriander*

5 kemiri nuts, crushed
3 teaspoons sugar
2 teaspoons salt
½ teaspoon shrimp (sauce) paste (see page 13)
One 4- to 4½-pound duck
1 cup fresh-grated coconut
5 pieces of jeruk purut, or 5 square inches of lemon peel (see page 12)
2 slices kencur (¼ teaspoon), soaked in 1 tablespoon water for thirty minutes (optional)
3 salam leaves
3 pieces of laos

1. In the blender, prepare a sauce of 1 cup of the coconut milk, the onion, garlic, tamarind liquid, chili, cumin, coriander, kemiri, sugar, salt and shrimp paste.
2. Cut the liver and heart of the duck into ½-inch pieces.
3. Mix one-half of the sauce with the giblets and grated coconut. Stuff the duck with this mixture, and sew up the cavity.
4. Put the duck in a large saucepan with the remaining coconut milk (3 cups), the balance of the sauce, the jeruk purut, kencur, salam and laos. Cover the pan, and cook over medium heat for about one and a half hours, or until the duck is tender. Baste frequently. When done, the sauce will have thickened considerably.

Note: At this stage, it is recommended that the duck be refrigerated for several hours or overnight. The congealed fat which has accumulated can then be lifted out easily and discarded. When ready to dine, proceed with the last step in the preparation.

5. Remove the duck and sauce to a roasting pan, and roast in a 400-degree oven, basting occasionally, for thirty minutes, or until the duck is crispy brown. Carve the duck into generous portions, and serve with the sauce and coconut stuffing.

Serves 6, with other dishes

Mostly Beef

Karangmenanci

BEEF STEW WITH SWEET SOY SAUCE

(JAVA)

Karangmenanci *exemplifies the regional taste of Java and is also an example* par excellence *of the Chinese heredity married to the Indonesian genius for stamping its identity on a borrowed recipe. The result has proved to be one of the most popular concoctions in my American kitchen* rijsttafel. *Pungent and sweet, slightly acid and with considerable character and dimension,* Karangmenanci *is guaranteed to please.*

It can be prepared in advance and kept for up to two days in the refrigerator, or frozen until needed. It should be thawed at room temperature for two hours before reheating.

1 pound boneless chuck, cut into 2-inch cubes
1 large clove garlic, sliced thin
¼ cup thin-sliced onion
2 fresh green semihot chilies, sliced thin
1 large slice ginger (about 1 teaspoon)
1 salam leaf
1 piece of laos
1 tablespoon peanut or corn oil
3 tablespoons sweet soy sauce (see page 237)
1 teaspoon sugar
1 teaspoon salt
2 tablespoons vinegar
1 cup water

1. In a large saucepan combine the beef, garlic, onion, chilies, ginger, salam, laos and oil. Fry for three minutes over medium heat.

2. Then add the sweet soy sauce, sugar, salt, vinegar and water, mix well and continue to cook in a covered pan for about one hour, or until the beef is tender and almost all the sauce has evaporated. Add ½ cup water should the beef become too dry during the cooking process.

Serves 6, with other dishes

❁

Semur Daging Jawa
AROMATIC BEEF FROM JAVA

The inclusion of pepper, nutmeg, clove, sweet soy sauce and sugar identifies the Semur *of Java. Actually* Semur *can be translated as "braise" or "stew" but implying the flavors noted. Aromatic and scented, with a passing nod to the apparently insatiable sweet tooth of the Javanese, this beef* Semur *has become one of the sought-after preparations in my kitchen. It can be prepared well in advance and kept in the refrigerator for up to two days, or frozen until needed. Thaw at room temperature for two hours before reheating.*

- ¼ cup sliced onion
- 1 tablespoon peanut or corn oil
- 1 pound boneless beef chuck, cut into 2-inch cubes
- 1 large slice ginger (about 2 teaspoons)
- 1 teaspoon salt
- ¼ teaspoon nutmeg
- ⅛ teaspoon ground cloves
- 1 cup water
- 2 tablespoons sweet soy sauce (see page 237)
- 1 teaspoon sugar
- 1 salam leaf
- 1 piece of laos
- 1 teaspoon vinegar
- ¼ teaspoon pepper

1. Fry the onion in the oil for one minute. Add the beef cubes, ginger, salt, nutmeg and cloves, and fry for three minutes.

2. Add the water, sweet soy sauce, sugar, salam, laos, vinegar and pepper. Mix well, and cook for about one hour, or until the meat has become tender and the sauce has thickened. If the sauce dries out too quickly, add ½ cup water during the cooking process.

Serves 6, with other dishes

Dendeng Ragi

SLICED BEEF WITH SHREDDED COCONUT

(SOLO, JAVA)

This rich and hearty beef, reinforced by the browned coconut shreds, is eaten at room temperature. It refrigerates very well for several days or more and is tasty when reheated. Traditionally the Dendeng *is eaten with ample white rice and seasoned with sweet soy sauce (see page 237).*

¼ cup sliced onion
3 cloves garlic, sliced
1 teaspoon ground cumin
1 tablespoon coriander
¼ cup coconut milk (see page 15)
1 pound round steak or chuck, sliced thin in 2-inch squares
2 cups fresh-grated coconut

2 teaspoons sugar
2 teaspoons salt
1 teaspoon tamarind, dissolved in 1 tablespoon water
¼ cup peanut or corn oil
2 salam leaves
2 pieces of laos
2 pieces of jeruk purut, or 2 square inches of lemon peel (*see page 12*)

1. In the blender, make a paste of the onion, garlic, cumin, coriander and coconut milk. Add it to the beef, coconut, sugar, salt and tamarind liquid. Mix well, and fry for five minutes.

2. Then add the oil, salam, laos and jeruk purut, and fry over medium heat for about thirty minutes, or until the meat and coconut are well browned and dry.

3. Squeeze the excess oil from the mixture, and turn it out on several thicknesses of paper towels. Allow to drain well.

Serves 6, with other dishes

❁

Besengek Daging
BEEF IN ASSORTED SPICES
(JAVA)

This dish may be made in advance and refrigerated for two days, or frozen until needed. Thaw at room temperature for two hours before reheating.

- 1 cup coconut milk (see page 15)
- 2 teaspoons tamarind, dissolved in 1 tablespoon water
- ¼ cup sliced onion
- 4 cloves garlic, sliced
- 4 kemiri nuts, crushed
- 2 teaspoons dried red hot chili
- 2 teaspoons coriander
- ¼ teaspoon turmeric
- 1 teaspoon salt
- ½ teaspoon sugar
- ¼ teaspoon shrimp (sauce) paste (see page 13)
- 1½ pounds beef chuck, cut into 1-inch cubes
- 1 salam leaf
- 1 piece of laos
- 1 stalk lemon grass
- ½ cup water (as needed)

1. Blend into a paste the coconut milk, tamarind liquid, onion, garlic, kemiri, chili, coriander, turmeric, salt, sugar and shrimp paste.

2. Pour the sauce into a saucepan, and bring to a boil. Add the beef, salam, laos and lemon grass. Cook for about one hour, or until the beef is tender. Add the water during cooking if the sauce should evaporate too quickly. The *Besengek* is served with its own thick sauce.
Serves 6, with other dishes

Lapis Daging Bogor
SLICED STEAK FRY
(BOGOR, WEST JAVA)

Bogor is the mountain retreat in West Java where the presidential palace is located. It was formerly known as Buitenzorg, where the Dutch established the great botanical garden and research center.

- ***½ pound flank or sirloin steak, sliced thin***
- ***1 egg, beaten***
- ***¼ cup thin-sliced onion***
- ***1 clove garlic, sliced thin***
- ***1 tablespoon butter***
- ***¼ cup water***
- ***1 tablespoon sweet soy sauce*** *(see page 237)*
- ***1 1-inch cinnamon stick***
- ***⅛ teaspoon ground cloves***
- ***⅛ teaspoon pepper***
- ***¼ cup coarse-chopped tomato***

Coat the steak slices with the beaten egg. Fry the onion and garlic in the butter for two minutes. Add the steak, and fry for two minutes more, or until the pink color begins to change. Then add the water, sweet soy sauce, cinnamon, cloves, pepper and tomato. Mix well, and continue to fry for five minutes, or until the sauce has thickened.

Serves 4, with other dishes

Kare Kol
CABBAGE AND BEEF CURRY
(CENTRAL JAVA)

1 pound beef chuck, cut into 4 pieces
2 cups water
¼ cup thin-sliced onion
2 cloves garlic, sliced
2 kemiri nuts, crushed
2 teaspoons coriander
2 teaspoons salt
¼ teaspoon turmeric
1 tablespoon peanut or corn oil
3 cups coarse-sliced cabbage
½ teaspoon sugar
1 stalk lemon grass
1 teaspoon tamarind, dissolved in 1 tablespoon water
1 cup coconut milk (*see page 15*)
2 pieces of laos

One 3-ounce package cellophane noodles

1. Boil the beef in the water for twenty minutes. Remove, and cut it into 1-inch cubes. Reserve the liquid.

2. Crush into a paste the onion, garlic, kemiri, coriander, salt and turmeric. Fry the paste in the oil for one minute, add the cabbage and fry for two minutes more, mixing well. Then add the beef, 1 cup of the reserved cooking liquid, the sugar, lemon grass, tamarind liquid, coconut milk and laos.

3. Cook the curry in a covered pan for about twenty minutes, or until the beef is tender. At this stage, add the cellophane noodles, and cook for five minutes more, mixing well to distribute the noodles.

Serves 6, with other dishes

Be Genjol
BALI BEEF
(BALI)

This dish may be cooked in advance and stored in the refrigerator for up to two days, or frozen until needed. Thaw at room temperature for two hours before reheating.

5 kemiri nuts, crushed
3 cloves garlic, sliced
¼ cup thin-sliced onion
¼ teaspoon turmeric
2 fresh red semihot chilies, sliced
¼ teaspoon shrimp (sauce) paste (see page 13)
¼ teaspoon ground cloves
¼ teaspoon pepper

1 slice ginger—about 1 teaspoon
2 teaspoons salt
3 cups water
2 pounds boneless chuck or round steak, cut into 2-inch cubes
2 salam leaves
1 piece of laos
2 slices kencur (1/4 teaspoon), soaked in water for fifteen minutes (optional)

1. Blend the kemiri, garlic, onion, turmeric, chilies, shrimp paste, cloves, pepper, ginger, salt and 1 cup of the water into a paste.

2. Marinate the beef cubes in the paste for fifteen minutes. Then cook the beef, salam, laos, kencur and the balance of the water (2 cups), in a covered saucepan for about one and a half hours, or until tender. Much of the liquid will have evaporated, leaving a thick sauce.

Variation: Bali is a Hindu island, so it is permissible for the Balinese to eat pork. The original recipe for *Be Genjol* called for boneless pork cubes. This too can be prepared in advance and refrigerated or frozen.
Serves 8, with other dishes

❂

Asam Pade Daging
HOT AND SOUR BEEF
(SUMATRA)

This is a hot and sour beef which exemplifies the truly Sumatran style of cooking. It is in sharp contrast with the foods of Java, which are often richly sweet and hot. The predominant acid flavor is provided by the popular, and sometimes indispensable, leguminous brown pulp found in the seedpods of the tamarind tree. The ripened pods have a soft, loose shell which is removed, and the pulp is soaked in water to separate the seeds and fibrous strings. The tamarind liquid imparts a pleasant acid flavor to the curries of India as well as to a host of meat, fish and vegetable dishes in Indonesia.

This dish may be prepared in advance and refrigerated for up to two days, or frozen until needed. Thaw for two hours at room temperature before reheating.

- **2** ***pounds boneless beef chuck or round steak, cut into 1-inch cubes***
- **1/4** ***cup thin-sliced onion***
- **5** ***cloves garlic, sliced thin***
- **1** ***piece of laos***
- **2** ***salam leaves***
- **1** ***slice fresh ginger (about 1 teaspoon)***
- **1/2** ***teaspoon turmeric***
- **2** ***teaspoons salt***
- **1** ***stalk lemon grass***
- **6** ***kemiri nuts, crushed***

1 tablespoon crushed fresh or dried red hot chili
2 tablespoons tamarind, dissolved in 3 tablespoons water
4 cups water

Cook all the ingredients together in a covered saucepan for about one and a half hours, or until the beef is tender but not overcooked. When done, there should be about 1 cup of the sauce left. Stir occasionally during cooking to distribute the flavors.
Serves 6, with other dishes

Sambal Blado
CRISPY CRUNCHY BEEF
(SUMATRA)

The Blado *has an unexpected chewy texture, which derives from the well-done beef slices. It is an admirable accompaniment to a* rijsttafel *where a contrast in textures is planned. The sauce is red hot! To make a sauce that is red hot but not so pungent, blend ¼ cup red sweet pepper with 2 tablespoons hot chili in ½ cup water. The sweet pepper provides a bright red color and dilutes the intense spiciness of the chili—the best of both worlds.*

2 pounds beef round steak or boneless chuck
2 cups water
7 tablespoons peanut or corn oil
½ cup thin-sliced onions
5 cloves garlic, sliced thin
3 tablespoons red hot chili, crushed into a paste
2 teaspoons salt
½ cup cubed ripe tomato

1. Cook the beef in the water for fifteen minutes. Remove, and slice into thin 2-inch squares. Discard the liquid.

2. Fry the beef slices in ¼ cup of the oil for five minutes or a bit more, or until the beef is brown and dry. Remove and set aside.

3. Fry the onions and garlic in the remaining 3 tablespoons oil for three minutes. Add the chili, salt and tomato, and cook for five minutes more. Then add the beef, and stir fry for five minutes to coat the slices and distribute the flavors.

Serves 8, with other dishes

Bumbu Bali Daging
SPICY BEEF IN RED SAUCE
(BALI)

The Bumbu Bali *has an attractive thick red sauce with an essentially spicy, somewhat pungent flavor. The red sweet pepper is added to give the sauce its vivid color and to dilute the sharpness of the hot chili.*

This may be prepared in advance and stored in the refriger-

ator for up to two days, or frozen until needed. Thaw for two hours at room temperature before reheating.

2 red semihot chilies, sliced
¼ cup sliced onion
2 cloves garlic, sliced
½ cup sliced red sweet pepper
2 cups coconut milk (see page 15)
1 teaspoon salt
2 teaspoons sugar
1 slice ginger (about 1 teaspoon)
2 salam leaves
2 pieces of laos
2 kemiri nuts, crushed
½ teaspoon shrimp (sauce) paste (see page 13)
1 teaspoon tamarind, dissolved in 1 tablespoon water
1 pound boneless chuck, cut into 1-inch cubes

1. Blend the chilies, onion, garlic, red sweet pepper and ½ cup of the coconut milk into a coarse paste.

2. Pour the sauce into a saucepan with the salt, sugar, ginger, salam, laos, kemiri, shrimp paste, tamarind liquid, beef and the balance of the coconut milk (1½ cups). Cook for one hour or a bit more, or until the beef is tender, basting frequently to create a smooth sauce.

Serves 6, with other dishes

❂

Den Den Unkep
DOUBLE COOKED BEEF
(SOLO, JAVA)

- 1 *pound sirloin or flank steak*
- 2 *teaspoons coriander*
- ¼ *teaspoon ground cumin*
- ½ *teaspoon salt*
- 1 *clove garlic, crushed*
- 2 *kemiri nuts, crushed*
- 1 *teaspoon tamarind, dissolved in 1 tablespoon water*
- 1 *salam leaf*
- 1 *piece of laos*
- ½ *teaspoon sugar*
- ¾ *cup water*
- 2 *tablespoons peanut or corn oil*

1. Cut the steak into slices about 3 inches long and ¼ inch thick.

2. Make a paste by combining the coriander, cumin, salt, garlic, kemiri and tamarind liquid. Rub the paste into the beef slices, and let them stand for fifteen minutes.

3. Add the beef, salam, laos and sugar to the water. Bring to a boil, and cook for about twenty minutes, or until the water has evaporated. Then add the oil, and fry, stirring frequently, for five minutes, or until the beef has browned. The *Den Den* can be eaten hot or at room temperature, but it's better hot.

Serves 6, with other dishes

❁

Empal
SPICY FRIED BEEF
(SOERABAJA, JAVA)

1 pound boneless beef chuck
2 cups water
1 teaspoon tamarind, dissolved in 1 tablespoon water
1 teaspoon sugar
1 teaspoon salt
2 cloves garlic, crushed
2 teaspoons coriander
¼ cup peanut or corn oil

1. Cook the beef in the water for thirty minutes. Remove and cut into 2-inch squares. Discard the liquid. Pound each piece of beef slightly to tenderize and flatten it.

2. Prepare a paste of the tamarind liquid, sugar, salt, garlic and coriander, and mix this with the beef squares. Let stand for fifteen minutes.

3. Heat the oil in a frying pan. Add the beef, and fry over medium heat for five minutes, or until the beef is brown and soft/crisp. Drain on paper towels.

Serves 5, with other dishes

Rendang

BEEF SPICE FROM SUMATRA

(JAVA)

This is a hot dish from Sumatra as interpreted by a friend from Java. More crushed chili, either fresh or dried, can be added, depending on one's tolerance.

If you like, the dish may be prepared in advance and refrigerated for up to two days, or frozen until needed. Thaw at room temperature for two hours before reheating.

- 2 *tablespoons chopped onion*
- 2 *cloves garlic, sliced*
- 1 *teaspoon salt*
- ½ *teaspoon turmeric*
- 1 *teaspoon dried red hot chili*
- 2 *tablespoons peanut or corn oil*
- 1½ *pounds beef chuck, cut into 2-inch cubes*
- 4 *cups coconut milk (**see page 15**)*
- 1 *slice ginger—about 1 teaspoon*
- 1 *piece of jeruk purut, or 1 square inch of lemon peel (**see page 12**)*
- 3 *salam leaves*
- 3 *pieces of laos*
- 4 *hard-boiled eggs, peeled (optional)*

1. Crush the onion, garlic, salt, turmeric and chili into a paste. Fry in the oil for two minutes. Add the beef cubes, and fry for three minutes more, stirring constantly.

2. Then add the coconut milk, ginger, jeruk purut, salam, laos and the whole eggs, if used. Cook over medium heat, basting frequently, for about one hour or more, or until the meat is tender and the liquid has almost completely evaporated, leaving a very thick sauce.
Serves 6, with other dishes

Rendang
SPICED COCONUT BEEF
(SUMATRA)

Rendang *is a hot, classic Sumatran dish rich in spices. It can be refrigerated for a week without altering its texture, or frozen indefinitely. It should be eaten at room temperature or warmed quickly under a broiler. The chilies are traditionally boiled in ½ cup water for ten minutes and then blended to make a bright red paste. However, for our purposes, the fresh chilies may be added directly without being boiled.*

1 cup grated coconut
½ cup thin-sliced onions
3 cloves garlic, sliced thin
¼ cup peanut or corn oil
¼ cup crushed fresh red hot chili
1 teaspoon turmeric
1 salam leaf
1 piece of laos
1 stalk lemon grass
1 teaspoon ground cumin

1 tablespoon coriander
1 1-inch slice ginger, cut into thin slivers
3 pounds boneless beef chuck or round steak, cut into 2-inch pieces
2 teaspoons salt
1½ cups coconut milk (see page 15)
2 teaspoons lemon juice

1. Toast the coconut in a dry frying pan over low heat, turning frequently, for about twenty minutes, or until brown. Crush it into an oily paste in a mortar or food processor.

2. In a large saucepan, fry the onions and garlic in the oil until light brown. Add the crushed toasted coconut, and mix well. Add the chilies, turmeric, salam, laos, lemon grass, cumin, coriander and ginger. Mix well.

3. Then add the beef cubes and salt. Cook over medium/low heat for thirty minutes. Then add the coconut milk, and cook for about forty-five minutes more, or until the beef is tender and the liquid has evaporated. Add the lemon juice, and cook a final ten minutes.

Serves 10, with other dishes

❁

Semur Daging

AROMATIC SPICED BEEF

(SUMATRA)

2 tablespoons sliced onion
2 cloves garlic, sliced
2 tablespoons peanut or corn oil
½ pound sirloin or flank steak, sliced into thin 3-inch lengths
½ cup beef broth or water
1 tablespoon sweet soy sauce (see page 237)
1 teaspoon salt
¼ teaspoon nutmeg

Fry the onion and garlic in the oil until light brown. Add the beef slices, and stir well. Then add all the other ingredients, and cook for ten minutes over medium heat as the sauce thickens. Serve hot or at room temperature. The *Semur* slices are also used as a garnish for the Sumatran *Gado Gado* (see page 191).
Serves 4, with other dishes

❂

Gadon

STEAMED BEEF AND COCONUT MILK

(CENTRAL JAVA)

The beef mixture for this dish is traditionally rolled in banana leaves and then steamed. Or the Gadon *may also be poured into a heatproof dish and steamed like a pie.*

1 pound ground beef
3 teaspoons coriander
1/4 teaspoon ground cumin
2 teaspoons salt
2 teaspoons sugar
1/8 teaspoon shrimp (sauce) paste (see page 13)
2 cloves garlic, sliced thin
2 tablespoons thin-sliced onion
5 pieces of jeruk purut, or 5 square inches of lemon peel (see page 12)
2 cups coconut milk (see page 15)

Six 2-inch pieces of salam leaf
Six 12-inch squares of aluminum foil

1. Mix together the beef, coriander, cumin, salt, sugar, shrimp paste, garlic, onion, jeruk purut and coconut milk.

2. Make a triangular pocket in a corner of a foil square. Hold the foil firmly in your palm, and add 6 tablespoons of the beef mixture. Fold the foil around the triangle, place one piece of salam on top and seal the edges in a more or less round shape.

3. Place the foil packages in a Chinese-style steamer for twenty minutes over medium heat. Unfold the packages, and serve individually, either hot or at room temperature.
Serves 6 to 8, with other dishes

❂

Sambal Goreng Printil
MINIATURE MEATBALLS IN COCONUT SAUCE
(JAVA)

- *1 pound ground beef*
- *1 teaspoon salt*
- *¼ cup peanut or corn oil*
- *¼ cup sliced onion*
- *2 cloves garlic, sliced*
- *1 teaspoon dried or fresh hot chili*
- *2 salam leaves*
- *2 pieces of laos*
- *¼ teaspoon shrimp (sauce) paste (see page 13)*
- *½ cup coconut milk (see page 15)*
- *½ teaspoon salt*
- *1 teaspoon sugar*
- *1 teaspoon tamarind, dissolved in 1 tablespoon water*
- *¼ pound snow peas*
- *2 ripe tomatoes, cut into 1-inch cubes*

1. Mix the beef and salt together, and shape meatballs ½ inch in diameter. Fry them in 3 tablespoons of the oil for two minutes. Drain, and set aside. They are now only partially cooked.

2. Fry the onion and garlic in the remaining 1 tablespoon of oil for two minutes. Add the chili, salam, laos, shrimp paste, coconut milk, salt, sugar, tamarind liquid and the meatballs. Cook for five minutes, basting frequently.

3. Add the whole snow peas and tomato cubes. Stir fry for five minutes more. Do not overcook.

Serves 6, with other dishes

Tahu Isi

STUFFED SOYBEAN CAKE

(JAKARTA, JAVA)

This festive party dish can be made many hours in advance and refrigerated until ready for the final steaming. The Chinese bean cake square is firmer in texture than the Japanese tofu *and is therefore more acceptable for our purposes. This dish is obviously of Chinese origin, but it uses ground beef instead of pork to conform to Islamic tenets.*

4 Chinese soybean cakes
½ cup peanut or corn oil
1 clove garlic
¼ teaspoon pepper
1 teaspoon salt
2 tablespoons chopped onion
2 eggs, beaten
½ pound ground beef

1. Fry the soy bean cakes in the oil about five to eight minutes, or until brown on both sides. Cut each cake diagonally

into two triangles. Scoop out about two-thirds of the soft interior, and mash it. Set aside the outer shells.

2. Crush the garlic, pepper, salt and onion into a paste. Add this to the mashed bean cake along with the eggs and ground beef. Mix well.

3. Stuff the eight triangles with the mixture, and smooth over the surface. Steam over hot water in a Chinese-style steamer for fifteen minutes. The steamed cake can be eaten in a simple chicken broth or as a side dish with a condiment of *Sambal Tomat* (page 244).

Serves 4 to 8, with other dishes

Semur Otak

BRAIN SAUTÉED IN SPICED SAUCE

(JAVA)

Indonesians are fond of brains, which can be a sometimes thing in the cuisines of other cultures. I have served many rijsttafels *which included* Semur Otak, *and without exception there was undivided enthusiasm for this aromatic preparation even from those who had previously considered brains beyond the pale. I urge you to try this culinary rarity which, because of the combination of island spices, predictably reflects the regional taste of the Javanese.*

1 pound beef brains
2 tablespoons chopped onion
2 tablespoons butter
3/4 cup water
1 tablespoon sweet soy sauce (see page 237)
1 teaspoon tomato ketchup
1 teaspoon salt
1/8 teaspoon ground cloves
1/4 teaspoon nutmeg
1/4 teaspoon pepper

1. Steam the brains over hot water for ten minutes in a Chinese-style steamer. Allow to cool, and slice into 8 to 10 pieces.

2. Fry the onion in the butter until light golden. Add the water, sweet soy sauce, tomato ketchup, salt, cloves, nutmeg and pepper. Stir well.

3. Add the brain slices, and baste several times. Cover the saucepan, and cook over medium heat for about ten minutes, or until the sauce thickens.

Serves 6 to 8, with other dishes

Gulai Otak
BRAIN CURRY
(SUMATRA)

1 pound beef brains
1/4 cup thin-sliced onion
2 cloves garlic, sliced thin

1 green hot chili, sliced open and seeds removed
1 tablespoon peanut or corn oil
2 teaspoons curry powder
¾ cup coconut milk (see page 15)
1 teaspoon salt
½ teaspoon sugar
2 salam leaves
2 pieces of jeruk purut, or 2 square inches of lemon peel (see page 12)
1 teaspoon tamarind, dissolved in 1 tablespoon water
½ green sweet pepper, sliced into long strips

1. Steam the brains in a Chinese-style steamer over hot water for ten minutes. Drain and cool. Cut into 8 to 10 slices, and set aside.

2. Fry the onion, garlic and the whole chili in the oil for two minutes. Add the curry powder, and stir well. Then add the coconut milk, salt, sugar, salam, jeruk purut and tamarind liquid, and stir for two minutes to blend the flavors. Now add the brain slices and the sweet pepper strips.

3. Cook, basting frequently, for ten minutes, or until the sauce has thickened.

Serves 6, with other dishes

❁

Gulai Otak

SPICED BRAINS IN COCONUT MILK

(SUMATRA)

1 pound beef brains
2 cups coconut milk (see page 15)
¼ cup thin-sliced onion
2 teaspoons salt
2 salam leaves
1 tablespoon fresh red hot chili, blended into a paste
1 stalk lemon grass
½ teaspoon turmeric
1 teaspoon ginger, sliced
¼ cup cubed ripe tomato

1. Cut the brains into 1-inch-thick slices, and remove the excess cartilage.

2. Bring the coconut milk to a boil in a frying pan; then add the onion, salt, salam, chili, lemon grass, turmeric, ginger and tomato. Cook for five minutes over medium heat.

3. Add the brain slices, and cook for fifteen minutes more, basting frequently. Serve hot or at room temperature.

Serves 6, with other dishes

Pepes Otak

STEAMED BRAINS IN WRAPPER

(JAVA)

Indonesians like to prepare certain foods in individual packages and then steam them. They are then unveiled and served. The wrapper, usually of banana leaf, serves as the plate and is discarded. Unfortunately we cannot step into our gardens and pluck an appropriate leaf, so we attempt the same thing with aluminum foil. The romance is gone, but the flavors are honestly served.

1 pound beef brains
5 kemiri nuts, crushed
¼ cup sliced onion
2 cloves garlic, sliced
2 teaspoons dried red hot chili, soaked in 1 tablespoon water
¼ teaspoon shrimp (sauce) paste (see page 13)
1 teaspoon salt
¼ teaspoon sugar
1 teaspoon tamarind, dissolved in tablespoon water
4 pieces aluminum foil, each 15 inches square

1. Steam the brains in a Chinese-style steamer for fifteen minutes. Cool, and slice into 12 pieces.

2. Crush the kemiri, onion, garlic, chili, shrimp paste, salt

and sugar into a paste. Add the tamarind liquid, and mix well. Mix the spice paste with the brain slices.

3. Place 3 pieces of brain in a square of foil, and make a package in the Indonesian fashion (see page 141). Seal the ends. Put the packages under the broiler for fifteen minutes, or bake in the oven at 375 degrees for thirty minutes. Unwrap, and serve.

Serves 4, one package each

Babat Goreng
FRIED TRIPE
(JAVA)

1 pound beef tripe
4 cups water, approximately
1 clove garlic, sliced
½ teaspoon coriander
½ teaspoon salt
¼ cup peanut or corn oil

1. Cook the tripe in water to cover for about one hour, or until it softens. Cut the tripe into 2-inch squares, and set it aside.

2. Grind the garlic, coriander and salt into a paste. Mix with the tripe squares, and let stand for thirty minutes.

3. Heat the oil in a wok or frying pan, and fry the tripe over medium heat for about ten minutes, or until it is brown and somewhat crisp. Serve hot or at room temperature.

Serves 8, with other dishes

❁

Lula Makassar

COCONUT LAMB SAUTÉ

(SULAWESI)

The Lula *is a specialty of Makassar city on the island of Sulawesi, formerly known as the Celebes. It may be prepared in advance and kept for up to two days in the refrigerator, or it can be frozen until needed. Thaw at room temperature for two hours before reheating.*

1 pound boneless lamb, cut into 2-inch cubes
1 teaspoon coriander
¼ cup chopped onion
1 teaspoon pepper
***¼ teaspoon shrimp** (**sauce**) **paste** (**see page 13**)*
1 teaspoon sugar
3 salam leaves
½ teaspoon ground cumin
1 teaspoon salt
2 cups grated coconut
***2 cups coconut milk** (**see page 15**)*

1. Fry the lamb, coriander, onion, pepper, shrimp paste, sugar, salam, cumin, salt and grated coconut together for about ten minutes over medium heat. Stir frequently.

2. Add the coconut milk, and cook for about forty-five minutes, or until the lamb is tender and nearly all the liquid has evaporated, leaving a thick residue of sauce and browned coconut.

Serves 4, with other dishes

❁

Gulai Kambing Padang
SUMATRA-STYLE LAMB STEW
(JAVA)

This Sumatra Gulai *was taught me by a lady from Java in whose home it was a specialty. It illustrates that some island foods do cross party lines, although there is a tendency to stick to one's own regional preferences. The entire lamb can be used in one form or another. All the meat, such as the tripe, heart, leg and shank, can be used to give a variety of textures to the dish. The* Gulai *spice* (Bumbu Gulai) *is a mixture of cloves, turmeric, kencur, coriander, pepper, anise, nutmeg, cinnamon, cardamom and cumin. The proportions are listed* *on page 129.*

- 2 *tablespoons chopped onion*
- 2 *cloves garlic, sliced*
- 2 *teaspoons salt*
- 2 *teaspoons dried red chili, soaked in 2 tablespoons water*
- 1 *teaspoon tamarind, dissolved in 1 tablespoon water*
- 1 *tablespoon* Bumbu Gulai (*see page 129*)
- 2 *tablespoons peanut or corn oil*
- 2 *pounds lamb (assorted cuts), cut into 2-inch pieces*
- ½ *cup water*
- 2 *salam leaves*
- 2 *pieces of laos*

2 stalks of lemon grass
1 piece of jeruk purut, or 1 square inch of lemon peel (see page 12)
1 teaspoon sugar
2 cups coconut milk (see page 15)

1. Crush the onion, garlic, salt, chili, tamarind liquid and *Bumbu Gulai* into a paste. Fry in the oil for about one minute. Add the lamb pieces, and brown for three or four minutes.

2. Then add the water, salam, laos, lemon grass, jeruk purut and sugar. Cook for about fifteen minutes over medium heat; then add the coconut milk. Cook for about forty-five minutes, or until the meat is tender and the sauce has somewhat evaporated. The *Gulai* should have a good quantity of sauce when done.

Serves 8, with other dishes

Bumbu Gulai
GULAI SPICE
(JAVA)

The Gulai spice combination is reminiscent of the five-spice mixture used in Chinese cooking. My cook in Calcutta also used in making chutneys or pickles, a five-spice mixture which was his own secret combination. Here is the Javanese Gulai *spice.*

1/8 teaspoon turmeric
1/8 teaspoon ground cloves
1/2 teaspoon ground cumin
1/2 teaspoon pepper
1/2 teaspoon star anise
1/3 teaspoon nutmeg
1/2 teaspoon cinnamon
2 cardamom seeds
1 tablespoon coriander

Mix all the ground spices together, and store in a jar with a tight cover.

Mostly Fish and Shrimp

❁

Sambal Goreng Udang
SHRIMP IN COCONUT MILK
(JAVA)

This recipe is an example of the classic Indonesian system of Sambal Goreng, *or stir-fried cooking. All the ingredients are prepared and collected in separate heaps. The oil is heated, usually in a Chinese- or Indonesian-style wok, and the ingredients are combined in rapid order. The frying time is short, which precludes overcooking, and the dish is served hot or at room temperature. A simple and painless method of cooking, easily integrated into the American kitchen.*

1 tablespoon peanut or corn oil
¼ cup thin-sliced onion
2 cloves garlic, sliced thin
½ green semihot chili, sliced thin diagonally
1 pound raw shrimp, peeled and deveined
½ cup coconut milk (see page 15)
1 teaspoon sugar
1 teaspoon tamarind, dissolved in 1 tablespoon water
1 salam leaf
1 piece of laos
1 ripe tomato, cubed

1. Heat the oil in a wok or large frying pan. Add the onion, garlic and chili, and fry for two minutes. Add the whole shrimp, and fry for two minutes more over medium/high heat.

2. Then add the coconut milk, sugar, tamarind liquid, salam and laos. Cook for two minutes, add the tomato and cook for three minutes more, basting frequently. Do not overcook.

Serves 4, with other dishes

Rebung Tjah

SHRIMP, STEAK AND BAMBOO SHOOTS

(SOERABAJA, JAVA)

Bamboo shoots and shrimp are a logical combination of the tropical forest and the sea. Driving through the countryside during my years of residence in India, I would pass tall, lacy stands of bamboo, and I understood their importance as food, timber and shade. Not all species of bamboo are palatable, although they may be edible. Those found in quantities in the markets of India and Indonesia were about 12 inches long and pointed, as though they had just emerged from the soil. The relationship between a fresh, crispy bamboo shoot and the canned variety is the same perhaps as chalk is to cheese. We must consider ourselves lucky, nonetheless, that canned shoots are now available all over the United States and that they give a good account of themselves, especially when used in the Rebung Tjah.

- ¼ **cup sliced onion**
- 1 **clove garlic, sliced**
- 1 **tablespoon salted black beans, crushed flat** (**see below**)
- 3 **tablespoons peanut or corn oil**
- ½ **pound shrimp, peeled and deveined**
- ¼ **pound flank or sirloin steak, sliced thin**
- ½ **teaspoon salt**
- ½ **teaspoon pepper**
- 1 **tablespoon sweet soy sauce** (**see page 237**)
- **One 6-ounce can bamboo shoots, sliced into matchsticks**
- 2 **tablespoons water**

1. Fry the onion, garlic and black beans in the oil in a wok or large frying pan for two minutes. Add the whole shrimp and the steak, and fry for two minutes more. Then add the salt, pepper, sweet soy sauce, bamboo shoots and water. Mix well, and stir fry for two minutes more.

Note: Fermented black beans are dried and salted preserved beans that are a popular ingredient in many Chinese dishes.

The beans are obtainable in any Southeast Asian food shop. I have stored mine in a jar with a tight cover on the kitchen shelf and am still using them after four years.
Serves 6, with other dishes

❂

Gulai Kacang Udang
SHRIMP AND STRING BEAN SAUTÉ
(SUMATRA)

This recipe is a vivid example of the Sumatran style in cooking. It is rich in spices, hot and acid. It contains no sugar and does not cater to timid taste buds. The combination of shrimp and string beans is imaginative. As in all Sumatran dishes, the amount of chili may be reduced according to your taste.

3 cups coconut milk (see page 15)
¼ cup sliced onion
3 cloves garlic, sliced
2 stalks lemon grass
2 teaspoons salt
2 salam leaves
1 piece of laos
1 teaspoon sliced fresh ginger
1 tablespoon crushed fresh red hot chili
1 teaspoon turmeric
1 pound string beans, cut into 2-inch pieces
1 pound shrimp, peeled and deveined
1 ripe tomato, cubed

1. In a large saucepan or wok, combine the coconut milk, onion, garlic, lemon grass, salt, salam, laos, ginger, chili and turmeric. Bring to a boil, and stir well.

2. Add the string beans, and cook for five minutes, basting frequently. Add the whole shrimp and the tomato, and cook for ten minutes more. When done, the sauce will thicken somewhat, and the dish is then ready to eat hot or at room temperature.

Variation: The long Chinese string bean, sometimes known as the asparagus bean, can be used in place of the ordinary supermarket variety. The long bean is popular with the Indonesians and can be easily purchased in Chinese or Philippine food shops.
Serves 8, with other dishes

❁

Pepes Udang
SHRIMP IN SPICY NUT SAUCE
(JAVA)

The Pepes *style of cooking means "wrapped in banana leaves." At the end of the cooking process the wrapper is opened, and the food placed under a broiler or hot flame, which gives a dry crust to the surface. Aluminum foil is our substitute for banana leaves, and it works well.*

- 2 *cloves garlic, sliced*
- ¼ *cup sliced onion*
- 1 *teaspoon salt*
- 1 *teaspoon dried red chili, soaked in 2 teaspoons water*
- ¼ *teaspoon coriander*
- ½ *teaspoon tamarind, dissolved in 1 teaspoon water*
- ¼ *teaspoon sugar*
- ¼ *teaspoon shrimp (sauce) paste (see page 13)*
- 6 *kemiri nuts, crushed*
- 1 *pound shrimp, peeled and deveined*
- 1 *salam leaf*
- 1 *piece of laos*

Aluminum foil

1. Crush the garlic, onion, salt, chili, coriander, tamarind liquid, sugar, shrimp paste and kemiri in a blender or mortar. Mix the spice paste with the whole shrimp, salam and laos. Make a loaf-shaped mound of the mixture on a piece of aluminum foil, and wrap it securely, making sure the ends are sealed.
2. Bake the foil loaf in a 425-degree oven for twenty minutes, or place the package under the broiler for the same length of time. Turn it over after ten minutes to cook the shrimp evenly. At the end of this step, open the center of the foil loaf 2 inches, and place it under the broiler for five minutes to form a brown crust.

Serves 6, with other dishes

❁

Sambal Udang Kantang
HOT SHRIMP AND POTATO FRY
(SUMATRA)

If you keep in mind the fact that the potato is a botanical immigrant from North America, this hybrid Sambal *makes a fine party dish, compatible with Western foods as well as with a* rijsttafel.

- ***1 pound potatoes, peeled and cut into ½-inch cubes***
- ***¼ cup peanut or corn oil***
- ***1 pound shrimp, peeled and deveined and mixed with 1 teaspoon salt***
- ***¼ cup sliced onion***
- ***1 tablespoon crushed fresh or dried red hot chili***
- ***¼ teaspoon salt***
- ***3 cloves garlic, sliced***
- ***¼ cup sliced ripe tomato***

1. Fry the potato cubes in the oil over medium heat for about ten minutes, or until they are soft but not brown. Remove from the oil, and set aside.

2. Fry the shrimp in the same oil for two minutes. Add the onion, chili, salt and garlic, and fry for three minutes more. Add the tomato and the potatoes. Mix well, and fry for two minutes more. Serve hot or at room temperature.

Serves 8, with other dishes

Tumis Kacang Panjang

LONG BEAN AND SHRIMP SAUTÉ

(JAVA-SUMATRA)

The long Chinese string-bean has a subtler flavor than the American supermarket variety. Tender, yet with a textured firmness, it is highly compatible when combined with the shrimp and traditional Indonesian spices and flavors in this dish.

- 2 ***kemiri nuts***
- ¼ ***cup sliced onion***
- 2 ***cloves garlic, sliced***
- 1 ***teaspoon dried red hot chili, soaked in 1 tablespoon water for 15 minutes***
- 2 ***tablespoons peanut or corn oil***
- ½ ***pound medium-size shrimp, peeled and deveined***
- ½ ***cup coconut milk (see page 15)***
- ½ ***teaspoon salt***
- 2 ***salam***
- 1 ***piece of laos***
- ½ ***pound long Chinese string beans, cut into 2-inch pieces***
- ½ ***teaspoon tamarind, dissolved in 2 teaspoons water***

Crush the kemiri, onion, garlic and chili into a paste. Fry in the oil for two minutes. Add the shrimp, and fry for two minutes more. Then add the coconut milk, salt, salam, laos, string beans and tamarind liquid. Cook for ten minutes, or until the beans are soft and the sauce has thickened.

Variations: Other vegetables, cut into bite-sized pieces, can be used as a substitute for the long Chinese string bean: cauliflower, supermarket string beans, zucchini squash, sliced celery or an assortment of several. I am particularly partial to the cauliflower and squash combination.
Serves 4, with other dishes

❁

Cumi Cumi Smoor
SPICED SQUID SAUTÉ
(SUMATRA)

Those who are longtime aficionados *of squid and addicted to its firm texture will find the aromatic sauce original and compatible. Those who have always been tentative about the pleasures of this ten-armed cephalopod may be won over.*

- 2 ***pounds fresh squid, cooked whole if small, or cut into 3- to 4-inch-long pieces***
- 10 ***tablespoons peanut or corn oil***
- ¼ ***cup sliced onion***
- 3 ***cloves garlic, sliced***
- 7 ***whole cloves***
- ½ ***teaspoon pepper***
- ⅛ ***teaspoon nutmeg***
- 3 ***tablespoons sweet soy sauce*** (*see page 237*)

½ ripe tomato, cubed
1 teaspoon salt
¼ cup water

1. Fry the squid in ½ cup of the oil for five minutes in a wok or large frying pan. Drain the squid, and set aside.

2. In another pan add the onion and garlic to the remaining 2 tablespoons of oil, and fry for three minutes, or until light brown. Add the squid and all the other ingredients—cloves, pepper, nutmeg, sweet soy sauce, tomato, salt and water. Cook for ten minutes more, or until the flavors have been distributed and the sauce has thickened slightly.

Serves 8, with other dishes

❁

Bongko Ikan Laut

STEAMED SEAFOOD ENVELOPES

(SOERABAJA, JAVA)

Banana leaves are used in Java for making steaming envelopes and are held together with wooden skewers. For our purposes, we use the serviceable aluminum foil, which can be twisted into any shape and sealed so that all the flavors are captured.

1 pound fillet of sole or flounder, cut into 3-inch pieces
½ pound large shrimp, peeled and deveined
¼ cup sliced onion
1 clove garlic, sliced
½ cup sliced ripe tomato

1 teaspoon dried red hot chili
2 teaspoons salt
½ teaspoon sugar
¼ teaspoon turmeric
2 teaspoons tamarind, dissolved in 1 tablespoon water
1 tablespoon water
2 slices fresh ginger (2 teaspoons)

Two 15-inch squares of aluminum foil

1. Mix all the ingredients together.
2. Make two steaming envelopes from the foil squares by distributing half the fish mixture in the center of each one and folding all four ends toward the center. Twist the ends together to seal. Steam over hot water in a Chinese-style steamer for thirty minutes. Open the envelopes, and serve in the foil.

Serves 6, with other dishes

❁

Pale Ikan

BAKED FISH IN COCONUT SAUCE
(SUMATRA)

2 pounds fillet of sole, cod or flounder, cut into 3- to 4-inch pieces
2 teaspoons salt
2 tablespoons tamarind, dissolved in ¼ cup water
¼ cup water
4 kemiri nuts, crushed
2 teaspoons crushed fresh red hot chili
2 teaspoons sliced ginger
2 teaspoons turmeric
¼ cup thin-sliced onion
3 cloves garlic, sliced thin
1 cup grated coconut
8 stalks lemon grass

4 20-inch squares of aluminum foil

1. Marinate the fish in the salt and the tamarind liquid for about thirty minutes.

2. In a blender, prepare a coarse paste of the water, kemiri, chili, ginger, turmeric, onion, garlic and coconut.

3. Take one square of foil, and make a layered package as follows:

1 stalk lemon grass, on the bottom
2 tablespoons spice paste
Cover with 1 slice of fish or 2 small ones
Cover with 2 tablespoons spice paste
Cover with 1 slice of fish
Then 2 tablespoons spice paste
1 slice of fish
Top with a stalk of lemon grass

Fold the foil over, and seal the ends with a firm twist. Complete this arrangement to make 4 fish packages.

4. Bake in a 375-degree oven for one hour. Unfold the foil, and serve hot.

Serves 4 to 6, with other dishes

Ikan Panggang
BAKED FISH
(SUMATRA)

Other fish that can be used to good account in this dish are red snapper and sea bass.

Two 1½-pound mackerels
2 teaspoons salt
2 teaspoons lemon juice
1 tablespoon dried red hot chili, boiled in 2 tablespoons water for two minutes
¼ cup thin-sliced onion
½ ripe tomato, sliced
3 tablespoons coconut milk (see page 15)
½ teaspoon turmeric

Aluminum foil

1. Score the mackerel four times diagonally on each side. Rub the fish inside and out with the salt and lemon juice.

2. In a blender, make a paste of the chili, onion, tomato, coconut milk and turmeric.

3. Place both fish on a large square of foil, and use a quarter of the paste to top both. Broil for five minutes. Turn the fish over, top with a quarter more sauce, and broil for five more minutes.

4. Turn the fish to the original side, top with the balance of

the sauce and broil for a final five minutes. The fish should be sizzling, and the top crispy. Eat hot.
Serves 4, with other dishes

❁

Mangut Ikan
PALEMBANG FISH IN COCONUT MILK
(SUMATRA)

Although the Mangut *has a considerable number of ingredients, it is essentially fried fish with a spicy Sumatran sauce. The turmeric tinges the sauce slightly yellow, while the pineapple and red and green peppers provide additional color. An altogether attractive, authentic and delicious fish dish. Palembang is a large city in Southeast Sumatra, where this recipe is reputed to have originated.*

1 pound sea bass or other, similar fish, cleaned, with tail and head intact
5 tablespoons peanut or corn oil
1 teaspoon dried red hot chili
1 teaspoon coriander
¼ teaspoon ground cumin
1 teaspoon salt
½ teaspoon sugar
¼ teaspoon turmeric
2 kemiri nuts, crushed
¼ teaspoon shrimp (sauce) paste (see page 13)
1½ cups coconut milk (see page 15)
¼ cup sliced onion
2 cloves garlic, sliced
½ cup red sweet pepper, sliced thin
½ cup green sweet pepper, sliced thin
½ cup fresh or canned pineapple cubes
1 salam leaf
1 piece of laos

1. Fry the fish in ¼ cup of the oil over medium heat for about three minutes on each side, or until it is crisp/brown. Remove and set aside.

2. In the blender, prepare a sauce of the chili, coriander, cumin, salt, sugar, turmeric, kemiri, shrimp paste and ½ cup of the coconut milk. Fry the paste in the remaining 1 tablespoon of oil for one minute.

3. Then add the onion, garlic, sweet peppers, pineapple, salam, laos and the balance of the coconut milk (1 cup). Cook for three minutes, stirring well.

4. Add the fried fish to the sauce, and cook, basting frequently, for five minutes. The sauce will thicken. Serve hot.
Serves 4, with other dishes

Acar Ikan
PICKLED FISH
(SUMATRA)

1 pound sea bass or red snapper, cleaned, but with head and tail intact
1/4 cup peanut or corn oil
1/4 cup thin-sliced onion
2 cloves garlic, sliced thin
1 fresh semihot chili, sliced thin diagonally
1 large slice ginger (about 2 teaspoons)
1/8 teaspoon turmeric
1 cup water
1 salam leaf
1 stalk lemon grass
2 teaspoons sugar
1 teaspoon salt
2 teaspoons vinegar
3 pieces of jeruk purut, or 3 square inches of lemon peel (see page 12)

1. Score the fish diagonally three times on each side, and fry in 3 tablespoons of the oil over medium heat for about ten minutes, turning once. The fish should be crispy but not dried out. Remove, and set aside.

2. Fry the onion, garlic, chili, ginger and turmeric for one minute in the remaining 1 tablespoon of oil. Add the water, salam and lemon grass and bring to a boil. Then add the sugar, salt, vinegar and jeruk purut. Cook for three minutes, add the fried fish to the sauce and cook for three minutes more, basting frequently, to reduce the sauce by half. Serve hot.

Serves 4, with other dishes

❁

Pepes Ikan
SPICY FISH BARBECUE PUFF
(ALL INDONESIA)

¼ cup chopped onion
1 clove garlic, chopped
½ teaspoon crushed dried red hot chili
¼ teaspoon shrimp (sauce) paste (see page 13)
1 teaspoon salt
½ teaspoon sugar
3 kemiri nuts, crushed
1 teaspoon tamarind, dissolved in 1 tablespoon water
¼ cup chopped ripe tomato
1 pound fillet of haddock, flounder or sole

One 15-inch square of aluminum foil

1. In a mortar or blender, prepare a coarse paste of all the ingredients except the fish. Cover both sides of the fish with the paste, and wrap envelope-style in the aluminum foil.

2. Place the envelope under the broiler for ten minutes; then turn over, and broil for ten minutes more. Open the envelope carefully, turn back the edges and place it under the broiler for five minutes to brown the top. Serve hot.

Serves 4, with other dishes

❁

Bumbu Bali Ikan

HOT SPICED FISH IN RED SAUCE
(BALI)

- 1 *pound sea bass, porgy or similar fish, scored three times on each side*
- 3 *teaspoons salt*
- 2 *teaspoons tamarind, dissolved in 2 tablespoons water*
- ¼ *cup peanut or corn oil*
- 2 *tablespoons chopped onion*
- 1 *clove garlic, sliced*
- ½ *cup water*
- ½ *cup sliced red sweet pepper*
- ½ *teaspoon shrimp (sauce) paste* *(see page 13)*
- ½ *teaspoon dried red hot chili*
- 3 *teaspoons sugar*

1. Marinate the fish in 2 teaspoons of the salt and half the tamarind liquid for fifteen minutes.

2. Heat the oil over medium heat, and fry the fish for about five minutes, or until light brown on both sides. Remove the fish, and set aside.

3. In a blender, prepare a coarse paste of the onion, garlic, water and sweet pepper.

4. Pour the paste in a frying pan, and add the shrimp paste, remaining salt (1 teaspoon), chili, the sugar and the rest of the tamarind liquid.

5. Cook the sauce over medium heat for ten minutes, or until the flavors have blended and the liquid is reduced to a thick consistency. Add the fish, and cook, basting frequently, for two minutes. Cover the fish completely with the red sauce, and serve hot.

Serves 4, with other dishes

Telor Ikan
STEAMED FISH ROE
(SUMATRA)

1 pound fish roe of red snapper, sea bass or mackerel
5 scallions, sliced thin
1 teaspoon chopped ginger
1 stalk lemon grass
2 fresh hot chilies, cut in half vertically, seeds removed
1 teaspoon salt
2 tablespoons water

½ cup cubed ripe tomato

One 15-inch square of aluminum foil

1. Place the fish roe in the center of the foil square.
2. Mix all the other ingredients in a bowl, and pour over the roe. Fold the foil envelope-fashion toward the center, and seal the two sides together. The two end pieces should be twisted tightly and turned over toward the center. The envelope is then shaped like a large sausage roll.
3. Place the envelope in a Chinese-style steamer, and steam for thirty minutes. To serve, unroll the envelope, and eat the roe hot.

Serves 6, with other dishes

Pepes Telor Ikan
STEAMED FISH ROE
(ALL INDONESIA)

1 pound fish roe (sea bass, mackerel, etc.)
1 clove garlic, sliced
2 green semihot chilies, sliced thin
3 kemiri nuts, crushed
⅛ teaspoon turmeric
1 teaspoon tamarind, dissolved in 2 teaspoons water
1 teaspoon sugar
1½ teaspoons salt
1 salam leaf, broken into several pieces
2 pieces of laos
¼ teaspoon shrimp (sauce) paste *(see page 13)*

Two 12-inch squares of aluminum foil

1. Mix all the ingredients together.
2. Divide the mixture in half. Place one half on one of the foil squares, roll it up and seal the ends to form a sausage shape. Do the same with the other half.
3. Steam the packages over hot water in a Chinese-style steamer for thirty minutes. Unroll the foil, and serve hot.

Serves 6, with other dishes

Vegetables for the Vegetarian

❂

Terong Kare
EGGPLANT IN CURRY SAUCE
(SOLO, JAVA)

India, in the form of Hinduism and Buddhism, exerted a monumental influence on Indonesia for about 1,000 years, from the fifth to the fifteenth century A.D. *The Indian religions were assimilated into the village life of Java, Bali and the other islands, and the great Buddhist shrine of Borobudur, constructed in the eighth or ninth century* A.D., *is a testament to the influence of the Buddha. Then Islam took hold, and now only archaeological ruins, devoured by the encroaching jungle, remind us of what went before.*

The Indians brought not only their religions but also their spices and foods. Cumin, coriander, ginger, pepper, mango, eggplant and curry were introduced and absorbed into the Indonesian way of life.

1 *pound eggplant, cut vertically into 6 pieces*
¼ *cup sliced onion*
1 *clove garlic, sliced*
1 *tablespoon peanut or corn oil*
1 *teaspoon curry powder*
1 *cup coconut milk (see page 15)*
1 *salam leaf*
1 *stalk lemon grass*
2 *pieces of jeruk purut, or 2 square inches of lemon peel (see page 12)*
⅛ *shrimp (sauce) paste (see page 13)*
1 *teaspoon salt*
½ *teaspoon sugar*

1. Steam the eggplant over hot water for ten minutes in a Chinese-style steamer. Remove, and set aside.

2. Fry the onion and garlic in the oil for two minutes. Add the curry powder, and fry for one minute more. Then add the coconut milk, salam, laos, lemon grass, jeruk purut, shrimp paste, salt and sugar. Cook for five minutes to distribute the flavors.

3. Finally, add the strips of eggplant, and baste for three minutes. The sauce will have thickened. Do not overcook. The eggplant should not be mushy.

Serves 6, with other dishes

Semur Terong

EGGPLANT IN SWEET SOY SAUCE

(JAVA)

1 pound eggplant
4 tablespoons peanut or corn oil
1 tablespoon sliced onion
1 clove garlic, sliced
½ cup water
1 tablespoon sweet soy sauce (see page 237)
½ teaspoon pepper
¼ teaspoon nutmeg
1 teaspoon vinegar
½ teaspoon salt
1 teaspoon sugar

1. Cut the unpeeled eggplant into ½-inch-thick slices, and then cut the slices in half. Fry lightly in 2 tablespoons of the oil for two minutes, or until light brown and softened. Set aside.

2. Fry the onion and garlic in the remaining 2 tablespoons of oil until light brown. Add the water, sweet soy sauce, pepper, nutmeg, vinegar, salt and sugar, and cook for three minutes to prepare the sauce.

3. Cook the eggplant slices in the sauce for two minutes to distribute the flavors. Shake the pan several times to mix but not mash the eggplant. Serve hot or at room temperature.

Serves 6, with other dishes

Terong Balado
BAKED EGGPLANT IN HOT SAUCE
(SUMATRA)

The Balado *is a completely vegetarian dish that is seasoned in the Sumatran fashion, yet can be integrated into a Western menu. Eggplant has a tendency to absorb a lot of oil during frying. This problem has been eliminated by baking the eggplant in quarters and preparing the sauce separately.*

1 *pound eggplant, quartered vertically, including the stem*
3 *cloves garlic, sliced*
2 *tablespoons sliced onion*
2 *ripe tomatoes, sliced*
1 *teaspoon salt*
2 *teaspoons sugar*
2 *teaspoons fresh or dried red hot chili*
½ *cup water*
2 *tablespoons peanut or corn oil*

1. Bake the eggplant in a 400-degree oven for about twenty-five minutes, or until soft.

2. Blend the garlic, onion, tomatoes, salt, sugar, chili and water into a coarse paste. Fry this in the oil for about ten minutes over medium heat to reduce the liquid and distribute the flavors. Pour the sauce over the eggplant, and serve immediately.

Serves 6, with other dishes

Terong Bakar

BAKED EGGPLANT IN SIMPLE SAUCE

(SUMATRA)

1 pound eggplant
1 cup coconut milk (see page 15)
¼ cup thin-sliced onion
1 teaspoon chopped ginger
½ teaspoon salt

1. Bake the whole eggplant in a 400-degree oven for about thirty minutes, or until soft.

2. In a saucepan, cook together the coconut milk, onion, ginger and salt for five minutes.

3. Remove the skin from the eggplant, but leave the flesh attached to the stem end. Pour the hot sauce over the eggplant, and serve.

Serves 4, with other dishes

Semur Terong
STEAMED EGGPLANT IN DARK SAUCE
(JAVA)

1 pound eggplant, cut horizontally in ½-inch-thick slices
1 egg, beaten with ¼ teaspoon salt
6 tablespoons peanut or corn oil
¼ cup thin-sliced onion
2 cloves garlic, sliced thin
1 cup beef or chicken stock
½ teaspoon salt
½ teaspoon sugar
¼ teaspoon nutmeg
¼ teaspoon pepper
***2 teaspoons sweet soy sauce** (**see page 237**)*

1. Steam the eggplant slices in a Chinese-style steamer for five minutes. Remove, and allow to cool.

2. Dip the eggplant in the egg, and fry in 4 tablespoons of the oil for two minutes, or until light brown on both sides. Remove, and set aside.

3. Fry the onion and garlic in the remaining 2 tablespoons of oil for two minutes. Add the stock, salt, sugar, nutmeg, pepper and sweet soy sauce, and cook for three minutes. Finally, add the eggplant, and cook, basting, for two minutes.

Serves 5, with other dishes

❁

Sayur Lodeh
EGGPLANT STEW
(CENTRAL JAVA)

The Sayur *is a stew that could be considered a soup since it does have enough liquid for both possibilities. It is served along with the other dishes in a* rijsttafel *in no particular order.*

1 red sweet pepper, cubed
¼ cup sliced onion
1 clove garlic, sliced
1 salam leaf
1 piece of laos
¼ teaspoon shrimp (sauce) paste (see page 13)
½ teaspoon tamarind, dissolved in 1 tablespoon water
¼ teaspoon ground cumin
½ teaspoon coriander
1 teaspoon salt
½ teaspoon sugar
1 kemiri nut, crushed
1 cup chicken or beef broth
1 cup coconut milk (see page 15)
1 pound eggplant, cut into 1-inch cubes

1. Put all the ingredients except the coconut milk and the eggplant in a saucepan. Bring to a boil, and cook over medium heat for five minutes.

2. Add the eggplant cubes and the coconut milk, and cook

for ten minutes, basting frequently. The eggplant should be soft but not overcooked.

Variation: Another possible vegetable combination for this stew/soup is to replace the eggplant with 2 cups string beans, cut into 1-inch pieces, and 1 cup shredded cabbage.
Serves 6, with other dishes

Suki Hati
HAPPY HEART
(JAVA)

Over the centuries a large group of ethnic Chinese has established residence in Indonesia, and their influence in the native cuisine has been profound. The Indonesians have adapted and absorbed the new foods combining them in new ways. Recipes that contain soybean cakes, sweet soy sauce and Chinese cabbage reveal their ethnic origin.

- *3 Chinese-style soybean cakes*
- *5 tablespoons peanut or corn oil*
- *¼ sliced onion*
- *2 cloves garlic, sliced*
- *¼ cup dried shrimp, soaked in ½ cup water for thirty minutes, then drained*
- *2 tablespoons sweet soy sauce (see page 237)*
- *1 teaspoon salt*
- *1 teaspoon pepper*
- *½ cup water*
- *1 pound Chinese cabbage, cut into 1-inch slices*

1. Fry the bean cakes in ¼ cup of the oil until light brown on both sides. Cut them into 1-inch cubes—9 to each bean cake.

2. Fry the onion and garlic in the remaining 1 tablespoon of oil for two minutes. Add the drained shrimp, sweet soy sauce, salt, pepper and water, and bring to a boil. Add the bean cake cubes, and cook for two minutes to allow them to absorb some of the sauce. Finally, add the cabbage slices, and stir well, cooking for five minutes. Do not overcook since the cabbage should be crunchy.

Serves 6, with other dishes

❁

Bumbu Rudjak Tahu

BEAN CAKE IN MIXED SPICE SAUCE

(WONOSOBO, CENTRAL JAVA)

The rich and pungent sauce is an excellent contrast with the bland cooked bean cakes which are elevated in this dish to a meatlike texture. The red sweet pepper or tomato provide flavor but are used primarily to tint the sauce an attractive pink color.

2 cloves garlic, sliced
3 kemiri nuts, crushed
2 tablespoons chopped onion
1 tablespoon crushed dried red hot chili
½ cup red sweet pepper or *1 red ripe tomato, sliced*
1 cup coconut milk (see page 15)
1 tablespoon peanut or corn oil
1 teaspoon salt
1 teaspoon sugar
2 salam leaves
1 piece of laos
1 stalk lemon grass
4 Chinese soybean cakes, cut in half and boiled in water for ten minutes

1. Blend the garlic, kemiri, onion, chili and sweet pepper (or tomato) with ½ cup of the coconut milk to make a coarse paste.

2. Fry the paste in the oil for one minute. Then add the salt, sugar, salam, laos, lemon grass, bean cakes and the balance of the coconut milk (½ cup). Cook and baste over medium heat for about ten minutes, or until nearly all the sauce has evaporated or been absorbed by the bean cakes.

Serves 6, with other foods

❁

Tahu Kering
SOY BEAN CAKE FRY
(EAST JAVA)

This unusual recipe will be appreciated by vegetarians and devotees of soybean curd in any form. The Kering *is a dry dish with a touch of sweet and sour chewy bean curd slices. It can be served with drinks before dinner or with other* rijsttafel *dishes.*

- 4 *Chinese soybean cakes*
- ½ *cup peanut or corn oil*
- 2 *cloves garlic, sliced*
- ¼ *cup sliced onion*
- 2 *semihot red chilies, sliced thin diagonally*
- 1 *salam leaf*
- 1 *piece of laos*
- 1 *tablespoon sugar*
- 1 *teaspoon salt*
- 2 *teaspoons tamarind, dissolved in 1 tablespoon water*
- 1 *tablespoon sweet soy sauce* (*see page 237*)

1. Cut the soybean cakes into cubes, ¼ inch thick and ¾ inches square. Fry them in the oil for five to seven minutes, or until they are light brown and dry. Do not overcook, or they will become too leathery. Remove, and set aside.

2. Remove all but 1 tablespoon oil. Fry the garlic, onion, chilies, salam and laos until brown. Add the bean cake slices,

sugar, salt, tamarind liquid and sweet soy sauce. Fry for five minutes more, or until all the liquid has evaporated and the flavors are distributed.

Serves 6, with other dishes

Tahu Goreng

FRIED SOYBEAN CAKE WITH PEANUT DRESSING

(KEDIRI, EAST JAVA)

Frying the whole soybean cakes in hot oil gives the outer surface a firm texture but allows the interior to remain soft and creamy. I have also, as a change of pace, cut the raw bean cake into nine cubes, dried them on a towel and then deep fried the cubes, thus providing more surface texture and, in my opinion, more dimension to the Tahu Goreng. *This dish is traditionally eaten with rice rolls* (Lontong) (*page 19*) *or plain boiled rice.*

- *4 Chinese soybean cakes*
- *½ cup peanut or corn oil*
- *1 cup fresh bean sprouts*
- *1 clove garlic, sliced*
- *½ fresh green hot chili, sliced*
- *1 teaspoon sugar*
- *4 tablespoons sweet soy sauce* (*see page 237*)
- *2 tablespoons water*
- *1 teaspoon lemon juice*

2 *tablespoons crunchy peanut butter*
2 *scallions, sliced thin*
3 *tablespoons crispy fried onions* (*see page 224*)

1. Fry the whole bean cakes in the oil until they are light brown on both sides. Remove, and set aside.

2. Blanch the bean sprouts in hot water for two minutes, and drain well.

3. In a mortar, crush together the garlic, chili and sugar. Mix into a fairly smooth sauce with the sweet soy sauce, water, lemon juice and peanut butter.

4. Cut each fried bean cake into 9 cubes, and put them in a serving dish. Cover with the bean sprouts. Add the peanut dressing, and garnish with the scallions and the crispy onions.

Serves 6, with other dishes

❂

Sambal Goreng Buntjies
SPICED STRING BEANS
(JAVA)

¼ cup sliced onion
3 cloves garlic, sliced
2 semihot red or green chilies, sliced thin
2 tablespoons peanut or corn oil
1 pound string beans, cut diagonally into ¼-inch slices
1½ cups coconut milk (see page 15)
¼ teaspoon shrimp (sauce) paste (see page 13)
1 teaspoon salt
1 teaspoon tamarind, dissolved in 1 tablespoon water
2 salam leaves
2 pieces of laos
2 cups cubed tomatoes

1. Fry the onion, garlic and chilies in the oil for three minutes. Add the string beans, and stir well for about two minutes.
2. Then add all the other ingredients, and cook over medium heat, basting frequently, for about ten minutes, or until the string beans are soft but still crunchy.

Variation: The long Chinese string bean is more tender than our North American variety. There are no strings attached to

this bean, and the cooking time can be reduced by several minutes. Taste the beans to prevent overcooking.
Serves 8, with other dishes

Tumis
QUICK STRING BEAN AND DRIED SHRIMP SAUTÉ
(JAVA)

Dried shrimp are not a substitute for fresh shrimp since they perform different functions. The dried shrimp in the Tumis *provide a mild shrimp flavor and an additional texture that contrasts with the ever-popular string beans.*

- **3 *tablespoons dried shrimp***
- **1 *cup water***
- **¼ *cup thin-sliced onion***
- **1 *clove garlic, sliced thin***
- **1 *tablespoon peanut or corn oil***
- **½ *red sweet pepper, sliced thin***
- **1 *cup coconut milk* (*see page 15*)**
- **½ *teaspoon salt***
- **1 *teaspoon sugar***
- **½ *pound string beans, cut into 2-inch pieces***

1. Soak the shrimp in the water for fifteen minutes. Drain well.

2. Fry the onion and garlic in the oil for one minute, add the sweet pepper and stir well. Then add the drained shrimp and

the coconut milk, and fry for two minutes more. Add the sugar, salt and string beans, and cook, basting frequently, for about five minutes or more, or until the beans are soft but still crunchy.

Serves 4, with other dishes

Sambal Goreng Bloemkool
CAULIFLOWER STEW
(JAVA)

The cauliflower was probably brought to Indonesia by the Dutch colonists, who simply could not do without their European vegetables. Once in Indonesia, the cauliflower joined its Oriental cousins, such as bok choy, Chinese cabbage and broccoli. Thus nostalgia for the home country (an unlikely reason) might be responsible for the dissemination of foods from one continent to another. But the cauliflower was welcomed and has been incorporated into many native dishes, including this one.

- ¼ cup sliced onion
- 2 cloves garlic, sliced
- 2 small fresh green hot chilies, sliced thin
- 1 tablespoon peanut or corn oil
- 1 head cauliflower (about 1 pound), cut into small florets
- 1 cup coconut milk (see page 15)
- 1 salam leaf
- 1 piece of laos

1 teaspoon salt
1 teaspoon sugar
¼ teaspoon shrimp (sauce) paste *(see page 13)*
1 teaspoon tamarind, dissolved in 1 tablespoon water
½ cup cubed ripe tomatoes

1. Fry the onion, garlic and chilies in the oil for two minutes. Add the cauliflower, and fry for two minutes more.

2. Then add the coconut milk, salam, laos, salt, sugar, shrimp paste, and tamarind liquid, and cook for five minutes over medium heat, basting frequently. Add the tomatoes and cook for three minutes more. Do not overcook since the cauliflower should be at the soft but crunchy stage.

Serves 6, with other dishes

Oseng Oseng Hijau
LETTUCE SAUTÉ
(CENTRAL JAVA)

***2** tablespoons chopped onion*
***2** cloves garlic, sliced*
***1** tablespoon butter*
***½** teaspoon salt*
***¼** teaspoon pepper*
***¼** cup water*
***1** head Boston or Romaine lettuce (about ¾ pound), cut into coarse chunks*

1. Fry the onion and garlic in the butter for three minutes. Add the salt, pepper and water, cook for a minute and add the lettuce.

2. Stir fry over high heat for three minutes more, or until the lettuce is wilted, but still green and with texture.

Serves 6, with other dishes

Oseng Oseng Sayuran
ASSORTED VEGETABLE SAUTÉ
(CENTRAL JAVA)

¼ cup thin-sliced onion
2 cloves garlic, sliced thin
2 tablespoons peanut or corn oil
2 cups coarse-shredded cabbage
1 cup string beans, cut into 2-inch lengths
1 cup carrots, sliced thin diagonally
½ green sweet pepper, sliced
1 teaspoon dried red hot chili
1 teaspoon salt
½ teaspoon sugar
1 salam leaf
***1 tablespoon sweet soy sauce** (**see page 237**)*

Fry the onion and garlic in the oil in a large saucepan for two minutes. Add all the other ingredients, and stir fry for five to seven minutes. The vegetables should be crunchy. Do not overcook.

Serves 6, with other dishes

❂

Oseng Oseng
SPICY SQUASH SAUTÉ
(JAVA)

¼ cup thin-sliced onion
1 clove garlic, sliced thin
2 tablespoons peanut or corn oil
½ cup ground beef
1 teaspoon salt
½ teaspoon pepper
1 pound zucchini squash, cut into 1-inch cubes
½ cup cubed tomato
2 tablespoons water
½ cup cellophane noodles

1. Fry the onion and garlic in the oil for two minutes. Add the ground beef, salt and pepper, and fry for two minutes more, stirring well.

2. Then add the squash, tomatoes, water and noodles. Stir fry the mixture for five minutes to distribute the flavors. Do not overcook since the squash should retain a crunchy texture.

Variation: Any of the summer squashes, such as the yellow and scalloped marrow, will respond well to this recipe.
Serves 6, with other dishes

Pare

BITTER MELON SAUTÉ

(SUMATRA)

Bitter melon is not a melon. It is a beautifully sculptured, elongated green gourd about 6 to 8 inches in length. I first became acquainted with the bitter melon in the New Market in Calcutta. An Indian friend was fond of the bitter flavor and, after rinsing the slices in salted water, ate them raw! The Sumatran treatment dilutes the slightly harsh taste and masks it cleverly with the coconut milk, tomato, shrimp and chili. The melon is a conspicuous item on the stalls of vegetable vendors in New York's Chinatown throughout the year.

- ***1** pound bitter melon (2 melons)*
- ***1½** teaspoons salt*
- ***1** cup coconut milk (see page 15)*
- ***¼** cup sliced onion*
- ***3** cloves garlic, sliced*
- ***1** teaspoon fresh red hot chili, blended into a paste*
- ***¼** cup dried shrimp, soaked in water for thirty minutes and drained*
- ***¼** cup cubed tomato*

1. Cut the melons in half vertically, and remove the seeds and membranes. Slice in half-moons. Sprinkle the pieces with 1 teaspoon of the salt, and let them stand for ten minutes. Wash and drain well.

2. Put ¼ cup of the coconut milk in a saucepan. Add the onion and garlic, and cook for two minutes. Then add the chili, the remaining salt (½ teaspoon), shrimp, the balance of the coconut milk (¾ cup) and the melon slices. Cook for ten minutes, basting frequently. Add the tomato cubes, and cook for two minutes more. Do not overcook. The melon slices should be firm and crunchy.

Serves 6, with other dishes

Oseng Oseng Pare

BITTER MELON SAUTÉ

(EAST JAVA)

The Javanese have added their own special brand of voodoo and transformed the bitter melon into a most interesting, odd-flavored vegetable.

- *½ pound bitter melon (1 melon)*
- *¼ cup thin-sliced onion*
- *1 clove garlic, sliced thin*
- *½ teaspoon dried red hot chili*
- *¼ cup thin-sliced red sweet pepper*
- *¼ cup water*
- *¼ teaspoon shrimp (sauce) paste (see page 13)*
- *½ teaspoon salt*
- *2 teaspoons sweet soy sauce (see page 237)*
- *1 salam leaf*
- *1 teaspoon tamarind, dissolved in 1 tablespoon water*

1. Cut the melon open vertically, and remove the seeds and membrane. Cut into ¼-inch-thick slices.

2. Fry the onion, garlic and chili in the oil. Add the sweet pepper, and fry for a minute more. Then add the water, shrimp paste, salt, sweet soy sauce, salam, tamarind liquid and melon slices. Fry for about five minutes more, or until the mixture is soft and dry.

Variations: The *Oseng Oseng* has a certain versatility. Broccoli, cut into 2-inch buds, and the long Chinese string bean, broken into 1-inch pieces, can be substituted for the bitter melon.

Serves 4, with other dishes

Peceli
PINEAPPLE SAUTÉ
(SUMATRA)

Peceli *may be described as a sort of chutney that can be eaten with Western foods as well as the spicy Indonesian dishes.*

- ***1 fresh ripe medium-sized pineapple***
- ***5 tablespoons light or dark brown sugar***
- ***½ cup water***
- ***2 tablespoons butter***
- ***¼ cup thin-sliced onion***

¼ teaspoon ground cumin
½ teaspoon coriander
¼ teaspoon nutmeg
10 whole cloves
¼ teaspoon cinnamon
½ teaspoon pepper
1 teaspoon red semihot chili, crushed into a paste
2 pieces of laos
2 tablespoons lemon juice
1 teaspoon salt

1. Peel the pineapple, remove the core and cut into 2-inch cubes. There should be about 4 cups.

2. Cook the sugar and water for three minutes to prepare a thin syrup. Set aside.

3. Melt the butter in a saucepan, add the onion and brown slightly. Then add the sugar syrup, cumin, coriander, nutmeg, cloves, cinnamon, pepper, chili, laos and, finally, the pineapple cubes, lemon juice and salt. Cook for ten minutes over a medium heat to distribute the seasonings.

Serves 10, with other foods

Sambal Goreng Bung

BAMBOO SHOOTS IN COCONUT MILK

(SOERABAJA, JAVA)

¼ fresh red semihot chili, sliced thin
½ fresh green semihot chili, sliced thin
¼ cup sliced onion
1 clove garlic, sliced
1 tablespoon peanut or corn oil
2 cups canned or fresh julienned bamboo shoots
1 cup coconut milk (see page 15)
1 salam leaf
1 piece of laos
¼ teaspoon shrimp (sauce) paste (see page 13)
1 teaspoon sugar
1 teaspoon salt
½ teaspoon tamarind, dissolved in 1 tablespoon water

1. Fry the chilies, onion and garlic in the oil for two minutes. Add the bamboo shoots and coconut milk, and cook for one minute.

2. Then add the salam, laos, shrimp paste, sugar, salt and tamarind liquid. Cook over medium heat for ten minutes, or until the sauce is reduced by half and the flavors are distributed. Baste frequently. Eat hot or at room temperature.

Serves 6, with other dishes

Ketimun Bistek
CUCUMBER STEAK
(JAKARTA, JAVA)

The Ketimun *would appear to be a modern method of cooking cucumber. Emerging from Indonesia's capital city, it smacks somewhat of the spotless stainless steel kitchen of an expert in Javanese nutrition. Needless to say, the aromatic cucumber slices have never tasted better and are an asset to any* rijsttafel.

2 medium-sized cucumbers, peeled
1 teaspoon salt
1 tablespoon butter
¼ cup sliced onion
½ green semihot chili, sliced thin
1 clove garlic, sliced
¾ cup water
1 tablespoon vinegar
1 tablespoon sweet soy sauce (see page 237)
¼ teaspoon nutmeg
¼ teaspoon ground cloves
¼ teaspoon pepper

1. Prick the cucumber with the tines of a fork in a dozen places. Rub them with the salt, and let them stand for five minutes.

2. Fry the cucumbers in the butter for about ten minutes, or until light brown and softened. Remove them from the pan, and set aside.

3. In a blender, make a sauce of the onion, chili, garlic, water, vinegar, sweet soy sauce, nutmeg, cloves and pepper. Fry the sauce for about five minutes, or until the liquid has evaporated by half and the flavors are distributed.

4. Cut the cucumbers into ½-inch-thick slices and pour the warm sauce over all.

Serves 4, with other dishes

Pepes Jamur
BROILED MUSHROOMS
(SUMATRA)

Mushrooms are something of an expensive rarity in the Indonesian kitchen. A friend from the island of Sumatra has told me that it was customary on their estate to grow mushrooms in the rice paddies after harvesting the rice. In Sumatra, banana leaves are used as a wrapper for the mushroom packages which are broiled on a charcoal fire. In any case, the locked-in flavors of the mushrooms and seasonings are as delicious as they are unusual.

1½ pounds fresh mushrooms, sliced
½ cup thin-sliced onions
1 teaspoon chopped fresh ginger
1 stalk lemon grass, sliced thin
1 teaspoon salt
3 fresh red or green hot chilies, sliced thin vertically
½ cup cubed ripe tomatoes
¼ cup water

15-inch squares of aluminum foil

1. Mix all the ingredients together.
2. Place 2 cups of the mushroom mixture in the center of each foil square. Fold all four sides toward the center, and seal to make a ball-shaped package with a flat bottom. Make 3 packages.
3. Steam the packages for twenty-five minutes in a Chinese-style steamer. Open the foil, and serve.

Variation: Broiling the foil packages for twenty minutes over charcoal or in the oven takes us closer to the traditional Sumatran method of cooking the *Pepes.* This dish would lend itself admirably to an outdoor summer barbecue.
Serves 6, with other dishes

❁

Oseng Oseng Jamur
MUSHROOM SAUTÉ
(SOLO, JAVA)

Oseng Oseng *may be translated as a quick stir-fried dish, no trouble at all to prepare.*

- *¼ cup sliced onion*
- *1 clove garlic, sliced*
- *1 fresh green semihot chili, sliced thin diagonally*
- *1 tablespoon peanut or corn oil*
- *½ pound fresh mushrooms, sliced*
- *½ teaspoon sugar*
- *½ teaspoon salt*
- *¼ teaspoon shrimp (sauce) paste (see page 13)*
- *1 teaspoon tamarind, dissolved in 1 tablespoon water*
- *1 salam leaf*
- *1 piece of laos*

Fry the onion, garlic and chili in the oil for one minute. Add all the other ingredients, mix well and stir fry for three minutes more. Serve hot or at room temperature.

Serves 4, with other dishes

❁

Orak Arik Jagung
SCRAMBLED CORN AND ASSORTED VEGETABLES
(JAVA)

2 ***tablespoons thin-sliced onion***
2 ***cloves garlic, sliced thin***
1 ***tablespoon peanut or corn oil***
¼ ***pound small shrimp, peeled and deveined***
½ ***pound ground beef***
1 ***green semihot chili, sliced thin diagonally***
1 ***cup shredded cabbage*** **or** ***broccoli, cut in 2-inch pieces***
2 ***scallions, sliced thin***
1 ***12-ounce can corn niblets, well drained***
¼ ***teaspoon nutmeg***
½ ***teaspoon pepper***
1 ***teaspoon salt***
1½ ***cups carrots, cut in 2-inch-long matchsticks***
2 ***eggs, beaten***

1. Sauté the onion and garlic in the oil for one minute. Add the whole shrimp and the ground beef, and fry for three minutes, or until the beef changes color.

2. Then add the chili, cabbage (or broccoli), scallions, corn, nutmeg, pepper, salt and carrots. Fry for five minutes, and stir well. At this point, add the eggs, and fry for three minutes more, or until the mixture is somewhat dry but not overcooked.

Variation: The original method of preparing the *Orak Arik* is to use fresh corn kernels cut from the cob. I would recommend that every attempt be made to use fresh corn when it is in season. Two cups of fresh corn niblets will fulfill the requirements of the recipe.
Serves 6, with other dishes

Sambal Goreng Tomat
TOMATO STEW
(JAVA)

- ***1** pound ripe but firm tomatoes*
- ***¼** cup sliced onion*
- ***3** cloves garlic, sliced*
- ***2** teaspoons dried red hot chili*
- ***2** tablespoons peanut or corn oil*
- ***1** cup coconut milk (see page 15)*
- ***2** salam leaves*
- ***2** pieces of laos*
- ***¼** cup dried shrimp, soaked in water for ten minutes and drained*
- ***2** teaspoons sugar*
- ***1** teaspoon salt*
- ***2** teaspoons tamarind, dissolved in 1 tablespoon water*

1. Cut each tomato into 4 or 5 cubes.
2. Fry the onion, garlic and chili in the oil for two minutes.

Add the coconut milk, salam, laos, shrimp, sugar, salt and tamarind liquid, and cook over medium heat for ten minutes.

3. Add the tomato cubes, and cook for three minutes more, basting frequently. The sauce will thicken in cooking and develop an attractive pink color. Do not overcook. The tomatoes should remain firm and retain their shape. Eat hot or at room temperature.

Serves 6, with other dishes

Sayur Manis
COCONUT CREAMED VEGETABLES
(SUMATRA)

Two Asian vegetables prepared in the Sumatran style give this preparation an exotic and authentic ring. Sumatrans believe that one should break the string beans because cutting them toughens the bean pieces. Since by nature I am a great respecter of tradition and believe that the culinary actions and reactions acquired by the native cook through many years of individual experience cannot be faulted, it would not occur to me to doubt that this is so.

- **2** ***cups coconut milk*** (***see page 15***)
- **3** ***cloves garlic, sliced***
- **¼** ***cup thin-sliced onion***
- **1** ***slice ginger*** (***about 1 teaspoon***)
- **½** ***teaspoon turmeric***
- **2** ***teaspoons salt***

3 fresh semihot red or green chilies, sliced open vertically
1 stalk lemon grass
1 pound long Chinese string beans, broken into 2-inch pieces
1 pound Chinese broccoli, tough stems trimmed and discarded

Put the coconut milk, garlic, onion, ginger, turmeric, salt, whole chilies and lemon grass together in a saucepan, and bring to a boil. Add the string beans, and cook for five minutes, basting frequently. Then add the broccoli, and cook for ten minutes more. Finally, add the tomato cubes, baste a few times and remove from the heat. Serve hot or at room temperature.
Serves 8, with other dishes

Acar
CUCUMBER AND POTATO SALAD
(SUMATRA)

The Sumatrans often produce surprising combinations that are unknown to the other islanders who have a tendency to prefer their own regional cooking. This is a hearty and nutritious salad for the vegetarian which can stand on its own merits. On the other hand, its inclusion in a rijsttafel *would add an uncommon touch.*

- 4 *large potatoes (about 1½ pounds)*
- ½ *cup peanut or corn oil*
- 5 *hard-boiled eggs, yolks and whites separated*
- ½ *cup smooth or crunchy peanut butter*
- 1 *teaspoon salt*
- ½ *teaspoon pepper*
- 2 *tablespoons lemon juice*
- ¼ *cup water*
- 3 *cups peeled and thin-sliced cucumbers*

1. Peel the potatoes, and slice them in long, thin pieces—about 3 inches long and ½ inch wide. Fry the slices in the oil until they are brown and soft. Drain well, and set aside.

2. Prepare the salad sauce by crushing the egg yolks and mixing them with the peanut butter, salt, pepper, lemon juice and water.

3. Slice the egg whites, and mix them with the cucumbers, potatoes and the sauce. Serve at room temperature. You may adjust the taste somewhat with more or less salt and lemon juice if desired.

Serves 8, with other dishes

❁

Gudangan (Urab Urab)
CEREMONIAL VEGETABLE SALAD
(JAVA)

Urab Urab *is an old recipe, one that may even be ancient since it is eaten during various traditional ceremonies such as child-birth or the remembrance of the dead. The long Chinese string bean, for ceremonial purposes, is cooked whole to signify long life.*

From a culinary point of view, the Urab Urab *has the identifiable Indonesian flavors plus the added bonus of the grated coconut.*

¼ pound fresh spinach
½ cup string beans or long Chinese string beans, cut into 1-inch pieces
2 cups fresh bean sprouts
2 pieces of kencur, soaked in water for fifteen minutes
½ teaspoon salt
½ teaspoon sugar
1 fresh red semihot chili, cut into thin slices
1 clove garlic, crushed
½ teaspoon tamarind, dissolved in 2 teaspoons water
½ cup grated coconut

1. Prepare the vegetables in the following manner: Blanch the spinach in hot water for two minutes, and squeeze dry. Boil the string beans for five minutes, and drain well. Blanch

the bean sprouts in hot water for five minutes, and drain well on a towel.

2. Crush together into a paste the kencur, salt, sugar, chili, garlic and tamarind liquid. Mix this paste with the grated coconut.

3. Toss the vegetables with the seasoned coconut until the salad is well mixed.

Serves 6, with other dishes

❂

Gado Gado

MIXED INDONESIAN SALAD

(JAVA)

The migration of foods is always a fascinating subject to me, especially if the introduction has been from another continent during an early period of history when transportation was by foot, canoe, sailing vessel, oxcart or birds. Indonesia was a crossroads for the Portuguese, Spanish, English and Dutch moving to their possessions in Asia during the period of great colonial expansion. Invasions, both military and peaceful, came and went in the fluid rhythms of a Europe awakening to the commercial possibilities of the Orient. Conquests of a commercial, military or religious nature did not occur in isolation, and when people emigrated, their traditions and foods came with them. It is logically arguable that the invention of Gado Gado *is a product of migration.*

Gado Gado *is the preeminent Indonesian salad and universally admired. It combines the vegetables of Europe, Asia and North America with the peanut from either Brazil or Africa, and it utilizes the seasonings of Indonesia to amalga-*

mate them into a celebration. The Gado Gado *should be presented as an important salad in a large round bowl in which all the ingredients can be displayed to good advantage. It should be liberally prepared and luxuriously served.*

THE SAUCE:

- 1 slice kencur (¼ teaspoon), soaked in 1 tablespoon water for fifteen minutes (optional)
- 1 fresh hot red or green chili, sliced
- 1 clove garlic, sliced
- 1 tablespoon light or dark brown sugar
- ½ teaspoon salt
- 1 cup coconut milk (see page 15)
- ¼ teaspoon shrimp (sauce) paste (see page 13)
- 4 tablespoons smooth or crunchy peanut butter
- 1 teaspoon tamarind, dissolved in 1 tablespoon water
- 1 piece of jeruk purut, or 1 square inch of lemon peel (see page 12)

THE VEGETABLES:

- 1 cup string beans, cut into 2-inch pieces
- 1 cup julienne-sliced carrots
- 2 cups shredded cabbage
- 1 cup fresh bean sprouts
- 1 cup cooked and sliced potatoes
- 1 cup sliced cucumber

THE GARNISH:

- 1 Chinese soybean cake, fried in oil until brown and cut into 9 cubes
- 1 ripe tomato, sliced
- 2 hard-boiled eggs, sliced
- 3 tablespoons crispy fried onions (see page 224)

1. Crush the kencur, chili and garlic in a mortar. Add the paste to a blender along with the sugar, salt, coconut milk, shrimp paste, peanut butter and tamarind liquid. Blend into a sauce.

2. Cook the sauce with the jeruk purut over medium/low heat for about ten minutes, or until it has thickened and the color has darkened. Set aside, and keep warm.

3. Blanch the string beans and carrots separately for three minutes to soften them. Rinse under cold water, and drain well. Set aside.

4. Blanch the cabbage and bean sprouts separately for two minutes. Drain well, and set aside.

5. Arrange the vegetables in layers in a large, round serving dish: cabbage on the bottom, topped by a layer of string beans, then carrots, potatoes, cucumber and bean sprouts on top.

Scatter the soybean cubes over the bean sprouts, and decorate the circumference of the serving dish with alternate slices of egg and tomato. Pour the warm peanut sauce over the salad, and sprinkle with the crispy onions. The *Gado Gado* is eaten at room temperature.

Variations: Other vegetables that can be used are cauliflower, spinach, or long Chinese string beans, blanched and drained well. All the vegetables should remain crunchy.
Serves 8, with other dishes

Gado Gado Padang
MIXED SALAD, SUMATRA STYLE
(SUMATRA)

Gado Gado *is versatile whether you prefer the Javanese or the Sumatran version. My inclination is to have my cake and eat it, so to speak, by using the sauce of one with the arrangement and variety of vegetables in the other. The Sumatrans have added a pungency to the sauce with hot chili and lemon juice, and more often than not my taste buds respond pleasantly to this stimulus.*

THE VEGETABLES:

- 2 *cups long Chinese string beans, cut into 1-inch pieces*
- ½ *pound fresh bean sprouts*
- 3 *cups shredded cabbage*
- 3 *cups cooked, peeled and sliced potatoes*
- 3 *soybean cakes, fried in oil until brown and cut into 9 cubes*

THE SAUCE:

- 1 *teaspoon shrimp (sauce) paste (see page 13)*
- 1 *teaspoon crushed fresh or dry red hot chili*
- 1 *cup coconut milk (see page 15)*
- 2 *teaspoons sugar*
- 1 *teaspoon salt*
- 1 *tablespoon soy sauce*
- 3 *tablespoons lemon juice*
- ¾ *cup crunchy peanut butter*

THE GARNISH:

- 3 *hard-boiled eggs, sliced*
- ¼ *cup crispy fried onions (see page 224)*

1. Cook the string beans in water for two minutes to tenderize them. Rinse in cold water, and drain well. Blanch the bean sprouts in hot water for five minutes, and drain well. If the green cabbage leaves are used, they should first be blanched in hot water for two minutes and drained well. The white center leaves of the cabbage are used raw.

2. Put all the sauce ingredients in a saucepan, and bring to a boil. Cook over medium/low heat for about five minutes, or until all the flavors are distributed. Add 2 or 3 tablespoons

water to the sauce if it appears too thick. Keep warm until ready to use.

3. In a large bowl or platter, spread the layers of vegetables: string beans on the bottom, covered by the cabbage, then the bean sprouts, potatoes, and the fried soybean cubes. Top the arrangement with the sliced eggs and as much sauce as you wish. Sprinkle with the crispy onions.

The *gado gado* is traditionally served with the potato and beef *Perkedel* (page 209) and various types of *krupuk* (page 203).

Serves 8, with other dishes

Acar
GARDEN SALAD
(JAVA)

¼ cup water
½ cup white or cider vinegar
1 tablespoon salt
3 tablespoons sugar
1 thick slice ginger, crushed
1 cup thin-sliced onions
4 cups shredded cabbage
1 cup shredded carrots
1 cup thin-sliced cucumbers

1. Blend the water, vinegar, salt, sugar and ginger into a sauce.

2. Add all the vegetables, and mix well.

3. Refrigerate for three or four hours before serving.

Serves 8, with other dishes

Acar Kuning

PICKLED VEGETABLE SALAD

(SUMATRA)

- ***1 tablespoon peanut or corn oil***
- ***2 kemiri nuts, crushed***
- ***1 clove garlic, crushed***
- ***1/8 teaspoon turmeric***
- ***1/4 cup water***
- ***1 slice ginger (about 1 teaspoon) crushed***
- ***1 teaspoon salt***
- ***1 tablespoon sugar***
- ***2 tablespoons white or cider vinegar***
- ***1 cup julienne-sliced carrots***
- ***1 cup string beans, cut into 1-inch pieces***
- ***1 cup sliced cucumbers***

1. Heat the oil in a wok or large frying pan. Add the kemiri, garlic, turmeric, water, ginger, salt, sugar and vinegar. Cook the sauce for three minutes to blend the flavors.

2. Add the carrots, string beans and cucumbers, mixing and turning for three minutes to cook the vegetables partially and absorb the sauce. Remove from the heat, and turn out into a bowl. Refrigerate for two hours or more before serving.

Variations: Color and texture are important criteria for this salad. Other vegetables that can be used are bamboo shoots, red and green sweet peppers and the long Chinese string bean. A combination of three or four different vegetables is necessary to give interest to the salad and provide a variety of flavors and textures.

Serves 8, with other dishes

Kederok
FRESH SALAD WITH PEANUT SAUCE
(BANDUNG, WEST JAVA)

1 fresh red or green semihot chili, cut into thin slices
1 clove garlic, sliced
1 teaspoon salt
2 small slices kencur, soaked in water for thirty minutes (optional)
3 tablespoons crunchy peanut butter
1 teaspoon tamarind, dissolved in 1 tablespoon water
2 teaspoons sugar
1 cup thin-sliced cucumbers
1 cup fresh bean sprouts
1 cup lettuce, broken into bite-size pieces

1. Crush the chili, garlic, salt, kencur and peanut butter in a mortar.
2. Add the tamarind liquid and sugar. Mix well.

3. Toss the sauce with the vegetables until well mixed. Serve chilled or at room temperature.

Serves 4, with other dishes

Rujak
SPICY FRUIT SALAD
(EAST JAVA)

The Rujak *is another example of the Javanese ability to take conventional ingredients, in this case fruits, combine them with the predominant flavors of tamarind and chili and produce a mouth-watering salad. Serve it with rice and any of the beef barbecues for an unconventional, thoroughly tasty meal.*

- **1** ***green pear***
- **2** ***cucumbers, peeled, halved and seeds removed***
- **1** ***firm green apple***
- **1** ***green mango (if available during season)***
- **1** ***large orange, peeled and divided into sections***
- **½** ***teaspoon dried red hot chili, soaked in 1 teaspoon water***
- **¼** ***teaspoon shrimp (sauce) paste (see page 13)***
- **3** ***tablespoons light or dark brown sugar***
- **½** ***teaspoon salt***
- **1** ***teaspoon tamarind, dissolved in 1 tablespoon water***
- **½** ***cut pineapple, cut into ½-inch pieces***

1. Coarsely grate the pear, cucumbers, apple and mango, if available. Remove as much skin from the orange sections as possible, and cut in quarters.

2. Crush the chili, shrimp paste, sugar and salt together with the tamarind liquid to make a paste.

3. Add the pineapple to the other fruits and the cucumber, combine with the sugar paste and toss well. Serve at room temperature.

Serves 6, with other foods

Asinan

FRESH VEGETABLE SALAD WITH SOYBEAN CAKE

(JAKARTA, JAVA)

Asinan, *an invention from Jakarta, Indonesia's capital city, suits my own philosophy regarding the usefulness of ethnic foods that are relatively unknown! You can take a recipe that includes a number of recognizable items, add several exotic seasonings and come up with a preparation that is versatile enough to be integrated into more than one cuisine.* Asinan, *which is in harmony with a classic* rijsttafel *as well as with something as American as fried chicken and roast beef, meets all these requirements.*

2 teaspoons dried red hot chili, soaked in 1 tablespoon water for half an hour
1 tablespoon dried shrimp, soaked in 2 tablespoons water for half an hour
½ cup water
1 tablespoon smooth or crunchy peanut butter
1 tablespoon sugar
3 tablespoons white or cider vinegar
One 8-ounce can chunk pineapple and ½ cup juice
1 teaspoon salt
2 Chinese soybean cakes, boiled in water for ten minutes and drained
2 cups bean sprouts
1 bunch watercress, trimmed and broken into 3-inch pieces
2 cucumbers, seeded and cut into half-moons

1. Boil the chili and shrimp for two minutes in their soaking liquid. Blend into fine shreds with the water.

2. Prepare the sauce by mixing the peanut butter, sugar, vinegar, pineapple juice, the chili/shrimp mixture and the salt.

3. Cut the bean cakes into ½-inch cubes. Add all the vegetables, the pineapple, and bean cakes to the sauce, and mix well. Refrigerate for one hour before serving.

Serves 6, with other dishes

Asinan

MIXED SALAD

(SUMATRA)

- *2 tablespoons diagonally sliced fresh red hot chili*
- *2 teaspoons salt*
- *4 tablespoons dried shrimp, soaked in water for thirty minutes and drained*
- *½ cup white or cider vinegar*
- *¼ cup water*
- *2 tablespoons sugar*
- *3 tablespoons smooth or crunchy peanut butter*
- *3 Chinese soybean cakes, boiled in water for ten minutes and drained*
- *1 cup carrots, cut into 1½-inch-long julienne slices*
- *1 cup cucumbers, seeded and cut into 2-inch julienne slices*
- *½ pound bean sprouts*
- *¼ cup roasted peanuts*

1. In a blender, prepare a sauce of the chili, salt, shrimp, vinegar, water, sugar and peanut butter.
2. Cut the bean cakes into ½-inch cubes.
3. Mix the sauce with the bean cakes, carrots, cucumbers, bean sprouts and peanuts. Refrigerate for one hour.

Serves 8, with other dishes

❁

Timor Acar

FRESH SALAD FROM TIMOR

The northern half of the island of Timor was a Portuguese possession from the sixteenth century until recent years. The Portuguese retained a firm grip on their territory even during the Dutch Colonial period. This recipe, which may or may not be of Portuguese origin, adds sesame seeds to a palate-cooling salad. It is an uncommon touch that is not intrinsically Indonesian.

2 *large cucumbers, sliced into about 3 cups*
1 *ripe tomato, sliced*
¼ *cup thin-sliced onion*
1 *cup fresh bean sprouts*
⅓ *cup cider or wine vinegar*
1 *teaspoon salt*
1 *teaspoon sugar*
3 *tablespoons light-toasted sesame seeds*

1. Toss together all the ingredients, except the sesame seeds, and mix well. Refrigerate for about one hour.

2. Just before serving, sprinkle the salad with the sesame seeds.

Serves 6, with other foods

Lotis

VEGETABLE AND FRUIT DIP

(JAVA)

- 1 *cucumber, peeled*
- 1 *sweet potato, peeled*
- 1 *apple*
- 1 *pear*
- ½ *teaspoon shrimp (sauce) paste (see page 13)*
- 1 *teaspoon salt*
- ½ *a fresh green semihot chili, crushed*
- 1 *teaspoon tamarind, dissolved in 1 tablespoon water*
- 5 *tablespoons light or dark brown sugar*

1. Cut the vegetables and fruits into diagonal slices, and arrange in separate piles on a serving platter.

2. Prepare a sauce of the shrimp paste, salt, chili, tamarind liquid and sugar. Serve the *Lotis* as an hors d'oeuvre, with each person dipping the vegetable and fruit slices into the sauce.

Serves 4

Fritters, Garnishes and Chips

One of the most useful and tasty groups of Indonesian foods, and one that can be easily integrated into the American kitchen, are the fritters (*Perkedel*), both soft-fried and crispy. Many can be made in advance in quantity and frozen, while others that are crispy retain their texture when stored in airtight containers.

The variety of *Perkedel* is large; ingredients can be either exotic or conventional, but always with the identifying touch of spice that separates the men from the boys. They can be used with confidence in either Asian or Western menus.

Garnishes have a special use in that they are generally sprinkled over rice. They are decorative and enhance the flavors and textures of other foods.

There are various types of *Emping*, or chips, that can be purchased in a dry, sticklike form and then deep-fried. In the hot oil they expand into crispy, dry chips flavored with a predominant ingredient, such as shrimp (*krupuk*), fish, rice or the nutlike malinjo, perhaps the tastiest of them all. For some unknown reason, the word *krupuk* is the generic term used to describe all these chips, although it actually does mean specifically the shrimp-flavored variety.

The chips are made with tapioca flour, eggs, salt, shrimp, fish, rice or malinjo nuts, depending on the type. The mixture is shaped into a roll, steamed over hot water, sliced and then dried in the sun. These are commercially produced and can be purchased in their dried form at Asian food shops.

Fritters

Perkedel Kepiting
CRAB MEAT CAKES
(SEMARANG, CENTRAL JAVA)

The Dutch Colonial period started in about 1602 with the establishment of the Dutch East India Company for trade in the lucrative spice market. The colonists brought with them new vegetables from Europe, such as the cauliflower, cabbage, string bean, potato and corn (via Central America). Their influence on cuisine is apparent especially in the preparation of fritters, which the Javanese accepted and made their own.

2 medium-size potatoes (½ pound)
1 cup flaked fresh or canned crab meat
2 eggs
¼ cup fine-chopped onion
½ teaspoon pepper
½ teaspoon salt
¼ cup peanut or corn oil

1. Boil the potatoes in their skins for about twenty minutes, or until softened but still firm. Peel and mash.

2. Mix together all the ingredients except the oil. Shape small, round cakes 1½ inches in diameter and slightly flattened. Brown the cakes lightly in the oil. Serve warm or at room temperature.

Serves 6

Sambal Goreng Kering

SWEET AND SOUR POTATO STICKS

(SOLO, JAVA)

The Kering *is a most unconventional preparation that can be treated as an hors d'oeuvre, served as part of a Western vegetarian lunch or included in a traditional Indonesian meal. It is versatile, adaptable, quickly assembled and very easy to enjoy.*

¼ cup thin-sliced onion
1 clove garlic, sliced thin
½ a fresh red hot chili, sliced thin

2 *tablespoons peanut or corn oil*
2 *teaspoons tamarind, dissolved in 2 teaspoons water*
1 *tablespoon sugar*
¼ *teaspoon salt*
1 *1½-ounce can potato sticks (about 1 cup)*

1. In a wok or frying pan, fry the onion, garlic, and chili in the oil until light brown. Remove from the oil, and set aside.

2. Pour off all but 1 teaspoon of the oil. Add the tamarind liquid, sugar and salt, and cook over low heat until the sugar is dissolved and thickened. Add the potato sticks and the fried onion, garlic and chili to the mixture, and stir well, frying for one minute more to distribute the seasonings. The sticks can be eaten hot or cold, but hot is better.

Serves 4

Bawan Kepiting

CRAB MEAT FRITTERS

(CENTRAL JAVA)

3 *eggs*
4 *tablespoons rice flour*
2 *cloves garlic, crushed*
2 *tablespoons fine-chopped onion*
½ *teaspoon salt*
½ *teaspoon pepper*
1 *cup flaked fresh or canned crab meat*

1. Beat the eggs, and add the rice flour, garlic, onion, salt and pepper. Stir in the crab meat.

2. Heat the oil in a frying pan, and over medium heat, drop in heaping tablespoonfuls of the mixture to shape round, flat fritters about 2½ inches in diameter. Brown lightly on both sides. Serve warm.

Variation: One cup of flaked, lightly steamed flounder or sole can be substituted for the crab meat.
Serves 4

Perkedel Kantang
POTATO FRITTERS
(MADURA)

4 potatoes (about 1 pound)
½ cup peanut or corn oil
1 egg, beaten

1. Peel and slice the potatoes about ½ inch thick. Fry the slices in ¼ cup of the oil for about five to seven minutes, or until light brown. Remove and crush in a mortar or food processor. Mix in the egg, and stir well.

2. Shape the mixture into oval fritters the size of an egg, and fry in the remaining ¼ cup oil until brown. Drain well on paper towels. These fritters are cut into quarters and traditionally eaten with the *Soto Ayam Madura* (page 47).
Serves 6, with other dishes

Gimbal Udang
SHRIMP FRITTERS
(WEST JAVA)

The Gimbal *is a celebrated dish from the district of Tjiandjur in West Java, a region famous for its beautiful and seductive women.*

2 eggs
5 tablespoons flour
½ cup coconut milk (see page 15)
3 scallions, sliced thin
1½ cups fresh bean sprouts
2 teaspoons coriander
1 teaspoon salt
½ pound small shrimp, peeled, deveined and cut into bite-sized pieces
¼ cup peanut or corn oil

1. Beat the eggs, and mix with all the other ingredients except the oil.

2. Heat the oil in a frying pan, and scoop up a large tablespoon of the mixture for each fritter. Fry for about three minutes, or until light brown on both sides. The fritters should be soft and crunchy.

Serves 6, with other dishes

❁

Perkedel

POTATO AND BEEF FRITTERS

(SUMATRA)

4 potatoes (about 1 pound), sliced thin
½ cup peanut or corn oil
½ pound ground beef
½ cup thin-sliced celery
1 teaspoon salt
¼ teaspoon pepper
2 egg yolks

1. Fry the potato slices in ¼ cup of the oil until light brown and soft. Remove from the oil, and set aside.

2. Cook the beef in a dry frying pan, over low heat until it changes color. Add the celery, salt and pepper, and fry for two minutes more. Discard the liquid that accumulates.

3. Crush the fried potatoes in a food processor or mortar, and combine with the beef mixture. Add the egg yolks, and stir well. Prepare the fritters in the shape of a large, slightly flattened walnut. Fry in the remaining ¼ cup oil until brown. This recipe makes 30 fritters, to be used as a garnish with the special fried rice (page 21).

Variation: Mashed boiled potatoes can be substituted for the fried slices. The potatoes, however, should be firm and dry when mashed so that the fritters do not disintegrate in frying.
Serves 10

Perkedel
POTATO AND BEEF FRITTERS
(JAVA)

This type of small fritter is most often used as a garnish for traditional rice or noodle dishes. For my purposes, however, I have found it equally successful as a standby hors d'oeuvre for a Western-style cocktail party.

- ***2 tablespoons thin-sliced onion***
- ***1 clove garlic, sliced thin***
- ***8 tablespoons peanut or corn oil***
- ***1 pound potatoes, peeled and cut into ¼-inch-thick slices***
- ***1 egg yolk***
- ***½ pound ground beef***
- ***1 teaspoon salt***
- ***½ teaspoon pepper***
- ***1 whole egg, beaten***

1. Brown the onion and garlic in 4 tablespoons of the oil. Remove, and set aside. Fry the potato slices in the same oil until light brown.

2. Crush the fried potatoes, onion and garlic in a mortar or food processor. Add the egg yolk, beef, salt and pepper. Mix well.

3. Shape the mixture into balls the size of a walnut, and flatten slightly. Dip the fritters in the whole beaten egg, and fry them over medium heat in the remaining 4 tablespoons oil

for about two minutes, or until brown. Drain on paper towels. Serve hot or at room temperature.

Variation: Mashed potatoes can be used instead of the fried ones. Boil the potato slices in water, drain very well and mash them. Complete the recipe as indicated above.
Serves 6, or more

❂

Perkedel Daging
GROUND BEEF PATTIES
(SUMATRA)

The Sumatrans have a generous way of seasoning beef. The Perkedel *are richly seasoned, and the fried onion and garlic slices used both in the meat mixture and as a garnish give these patties an extra dash of flavor.*

- ½ cup thin-sliced onion
- 6 cloves garlic, sliced thin vertically
- ¼ cup peanut or corn oil
- 2 pounds ground beef
- ¼ teaspoon nutmeg
- 2 teaspoons salt
- 1 tablespoon crushed onion
- 1 clove garlic, crushed
- 1 teaspoon pepper
- ¼ cup celery, including leaves, sliced thin
- 3 eggs, beaten
- 2 tablespoons sweet soy sauce (see page 237)

1. Fry the ½ cup onion and the 6 cloves sliced garlic in the oil until light brown and somewhat crispy. Remove and set aside, saving the oil.

2. Combine the beef with the nutmeg, salt, crushed onion, crushed garlic, the pepper, celery and eggs. Mix well, and add the fried onion and garlic slices.

3. Make the patties the size of a very large egg, about 2½ inches long, and slightly flattened. This should make 12 patties.

4. Fry the patties in the same oil for five minutes on each side, turning once. Then add the sweet soy sauce, and fry for two minutes more. Serve the patties hot, sprinkled with the balance of the fried onion and garlic slices.

Serves 6, with other dishes

Martabak

BEEF AND EGG ENVELOPE

(SUMATRA)

The Martabak *is not an egg roll but perhaps can be considered its Indonesian rival. Hearty and filling, the* Martabak *can be integrated easily into a Western cocktail party, a small Oriental lunch or a complicated* rijsttafel. *Furthermore, the stuffed envelopes freeze well, and I have made and stored substantial quantities in my freezer for future use. The* Martabak *should be thawed for one hour and reheated in a 400-degree oven for ten minutes, or until crisp and sizzling. Sweet soy sauce (page 237) makes an admirable dip.*

1 pound ground beef
4 cloves garlic, chopped fine
¼ cup thin-sliced onion
2 teaspoons salt
1 teaspoon pepper
½ cup carrots, cut into thin slivers ½ inch long
4 eggs
6 scallions, sliced thin
1 2-pound package egg roll skins (24 squares)
Peanut or corn oil for deep frying

1. In a dry saucepan, fry the beef, garlic, onion, salt, pepper and carrots together for about five to seven minutes, or until cooked dry. Discard any liquid that accumulates in the pan. Cool the mixture.

2. Beat 1 egg, add 5 heaping tablespoons beef mixture and 1 tablespoon scallion. Mix well. This is the envelope stuffing.

3. Place 2 tablespoons stuffing in the center of an egg roll skin, and fold two opposite flaps over toward each other so that one overlaps the other by ½ inch. Then fold over the two opposite ends to form a 3″ x 5″ package, and press down slightly to distribute the contents. The center folds must overlap so that the contents do not leak out. Continue to make the egg/beef mixture until all the skins have been utilized.

4. Heat the oil in a wok or frying pan to a depth of at least 2 inches, and fry the envelope on both sides until brown and crisp. Drain on paper towels.

This recipe should make from 20 to 22 Martabaks

Variation: The Javanese version of the *Martabak* is prepared technically in the same manner as that from Sumatra. But the ingredients and seasonings are different, and you may prefer this version.

1 pound ground beef
1 teaspoon curry powder
¼ cup thin-sliced onion
2 teaspoons salt
1 teaspoon pepper
1 teaspoon sugar
1 tablespoon oil
4 eggs
6 scallions, sliced thin
One 2-pound package Chinese egg roll skins (24 squares)
Peanut or corn oil for deep frying

1. Fry the beef, curry powder, onion, salt, pepper and sugar in a frying pan with the oil until the beef has changed color. Discard any liquid that has accumulated. Allow the mixture to cool.

2. Proceed to prepare the *Martabak* in the same manner as that of Sumatra by stuffing the skins, frying, draining and freezing should you wish.

Serves 24 or more, as an appetizer

Rempah Kelapa

FRIED COCONUT FRITTERS

(JAVA)

The coconut fritter is not a dessert. Spiced in the Indonesian fashion and deep-fried, it is surprisingly meaty and is admirably suited to serve as a garnish for a rijsttafel *or at a cocktail party. It also freezes well.*

- *1 clove garlic, sliced*
- *1 slice kencur (¼ teaspoon), soaked in 2 teaspoons water for 30 minutes (optional)*
- *2 teaspoons salt*
- *1 teaspoon sugar*
- *1 tablespoon coriander*
- *2 large eggs, beaten*
- *1 tablespoon cornstarch*
- *2 cups fresh-grated coconut*
- *½ cup peanut or corn oil*

1. Crush the garlic and kencur to a paste. Mix with all the other ingredients except the oil.
2. Heat the oil in a wok or frying pan. Take a heaping teaspoon of the mixture, and pat it into the shape of a slightly flattened football. Fry the fritters over medium heat until light brown on both sides. Drain on paper towels. Serve warm or at room temperature.

Serves 8, with other dishes

Perkedel Ikan Soerabaya
CHOPPED FISH FRITTERS
(SOERABAYA)

These fritters can be made well in advance and frozen until needed.

- *1 pound fillet of raw sole or flounder, ground into a paste*

½ cup fresh-grated coconut
3 eggs, beaten
1 tablespoon cornstarch
1½ teaspoons coriander
½ teaspoon ground cumin
2 scallions, sliced thin
2 teaspoons lemon juice
1 teaspoon salt
½ cup peanut or corn oil

1. Mix all the ingredients together except the oil.
2. Take rounded teaspoonfuls of the mixture, and fry in medium/hot oil until light brown. Drain on paper towels.

Serves 8, with other dishes

Perkedel Tahu
BEEF AND SOYBEAN CAKE FRITTERS
(JAVA)

These fritters may be frozen.

2 Chinese soybean cakes, mashed
½ pound ground beef
2 tablespoons chopped onion
2 scallions, sliced thin
2 eggs, beaten
¼ teaspoon pepper
1 teaspoon salt
½ cup peanut or corn oil

1. Mix together the mashed soybean cakes, the beef, onion, scallions, eggs, pepper and salt.

2. Heat the oil in a wok or frying pan over medium heat. Drop in heaping teaspoonfuls of the mixture, and fry for about three minutes, or until brown on both sides. Serve hot or at room temperature.

Serves 6, with other dishes

❂

Perkedel Lobok

STUFFED POTATO FRITTERS

(JAVA)

- 2 *potatoes (about 1 cup mashed)*
- 1 *zucchini or yellow summer squash*
- 2 *green sweet peppers*
- 1 *egg, beaten*
- ½ *pound ground beef*
- 2 *tablespoons chopped onion*
- 1 *teaspoon salt*
- ½ *teaspoon pepper*
- ¼ *teaspoon nutmeg*
- ½ *cup peanut or corn oil*

1. Boil the potatoes in their skins until soft. Peel and mash them.

2. Prepare the squash and sweet peppers by cutting them in half vertically, removing the seeds of the peppers and scooping out the squash.

3. Mix together the egg, beef, onion, salt, pepper, nutmeg

and the mashed potatoes. Stuff the vegetables with the mixture.

4. Heat the oil in a frying pan over medium heat, and fry the fritters for five minutes on each side, or until brown. Drain well. Serve hot or at room temperature.

Serves 4, with other dishes

❁

Rempah
COCONUT AND BEEF FRITTERS
(JAVA)

The Rempah *freeze well.*

- ***1 clove garlic, sliced***
- ***1 teaspoon coriander***
- ***1 teaspoon sugar***
- ***1 teaspoon salt***
- ***¼ teaspoon shrimp (sauce) paste (see page 13)***
- ***1 slice kencur (¼ teaspoon), soaked in water for thirty minutes (optional)***
- ***½ teaspoon pepper***
- ***1 cup fresh-grated coconut***
- ***½ pound ground beef***
- ***2 eggs***
- ***1 cup peanut or corn oil***

1. Crush the garlic, coriander, sugar, salt, shrimp paste, kencur and pepper into a paste. Mix the paste with the grated coconut and ground beef. Add the eggs, and mix thoroughly.

2. Heat the oil in a wok or frying pan. For each fritter shape

a slightly flattened football with 1 heaping teaspoon of the mixture. Fry over medium heat for about three minutes, or until brown on both sides. Drain on paper towels. Serve hot or at room temperature.
Serves 8, with other dishes

Tahu Perkedel
BEAN CAKE FRITTERS
(JAVA)

Soybean curd cake, or tahu, *originated in China about 2,000 years ago and was introduced into Indonesia with the first Chinese commercial pilgrims. It is one of the introduced foods that has been thoroughly integrated into the Indonesian way of life.*

High in protein, the tahu *can be boiled, fried, stuffed, mashed and combined with other foods. A versatile and complete food with a highly eclectic personality, it can be smooth, creamy, crispy or chewy, served hot or cold. This particular recipe may be frozen.*

2 Chinese soybean cakes, mashed
2 scallions, sliced thin
2 tablespoons fine-chopped onion
½ teaspoon salt
¼ teaspoon pepper
2 eggs, beaten
½ cup peanut or corn oil

1. Mix together the soybean cakes, scallions, onion, salt, pepper and eggs.

2. Heat the oil in a wok or frying pan, and drop tablespoonfuls of the mixture into the oil. Brown lightly on both sides for about five minutes. Drain on paper towels. Serve hot or at room temperature.

Serves 6, with other dishes

❁

Perkedel Jagung
CORN AND SHRIMP FRITTERS
(MADURA)

The introduction of corn into Indonesia is one of the miracles in the extraordinary dissemination of food crops around the world during the sixteenth century and afterward.

Corn (maize) is a North American grain that originated in the Valley of Mexico. It was brought to Europe by Columbus and again by the Spanish after the conquest of Mexico and Guatemala in the sixteenth century. From Europe, during the great Portuguese, Spanish, English and Dutch Colonial activities in Asia, it was carried to the new colonies, where it was metamorphosed from an essentially temperate-climate crop to one that was adaptable to the tropics. It was the Spanish in about 1625, who introduced corn to Madura.

The island of Madura is a rather bleak region off the eastern coast of Java. Tidal waves wash in the seawater to collecting pools, where it evaporates, depositing the salt, which is central to Maduran industry. Agricultural conditions there were not conducive to the cultivation of rice, and corn ultimately re-

placed rice as a staple food item. The Madurese took to corn like the proverbial duck to water, and it was only one step farther to its integration into the native cuisine.

Meanwhile, in Europe, corn was still considered principally animal fodder.

1 12-ounce can corn niblets (*about 1½ cups*)
2 tablespoons chopped onion
½ cup shrimp, cut into bite-size pieces
1 clove garlic, crushed
2 scallions, sliced thin
1 teaspoon salt
1 tablespoon cornstarch
¼ teaspoon pepper
2 eggs, beaten
¼ cup peanut or corn oil

1. Mix the corn with the onion, shrimp, garlic, scallions, salt, cornstarch and pepper. Add the eggs, and mix well.

2. Heat the oil in a frying pan, drop in heaping tablespoonfuls of the mixture and fry over medium heat for about five to seven minutes, or until brown on both sides. Serve hot or at room temperature.

Variation: The original recipe calls for fresh corn niblets. Cut the niblets from two or more ears of corn, and mix with the same ingredients as above.

Serves 6, with other foods

❁

Rempeyek Kacan
PEANUT FRITTERS
(CENTRAL JAVA)

Rempeyek *are a specialty of Purwokerto, a town in Central Java.*

This is an ingenious recipe, and the only one of its type that I have discovered in Indonesia. Sliding the peanut batter around the sides of a wok is a unique method of shaping the fritter. The result is a crisp, spiced fritter of irregular shape and uncommon flavor.

1 cup rice flour
¾ cup water
1 egg, beaten
⅛ teaspoon baking soda
1 clove garlic, crushed
2 teaspoons coriander
½ teaspoon salt
¼ teaspoon sugar
1 cup peanut or corn oil
1 cup raw peanuts, broken in half

1. Make a batter by mixing together the rice flour, water, egg, baking soda, garlic, coriander, salt and sugar.

2. Heat the oil in a wok over medium/high heat. Add one-third of the peanuts to the batter. This will be a thin mixture. Pour 1 tablespoon of the peanut batter against the side of the wok just above the level of the hot oil. Do this in tablespoon-

fuls all around the wok. Let the fritters fry a minute, scrape them off and let them float and fry in the oil for two minutes. When they are light brown, turn the fritters over and fry them on the other side for a minute. Remove, and drain on paper towels.

3. Add a third more of the peanuts to the batter, and continue the process until all the peanuts and batter are used. The fritters should be thin and crispy and about 2½ inches in diameter.

The *Rempeyek* are excellent cocktail party snacks. They can be made in quantities, drained, cooled and stored in tins or plastic bags to retain their crispness.

Makes 20 to 25 fritters
Serves 8, with other dishes

Perkedel Ikan
FISH STUFFED PEPPER
(AMBON)

The island of Ambon is reputed to be one of the islands in the Moluccas where nutmeg is historically indigenous. The Portuguese discovered nutmeg in the early sixteenth century, and the Dutch restricted its cultivation to Ambon in order to maintain their monopoly of the spice. Strangely, this Perkedel *does not contain a grain of nutmeg. Nevertheless, it is a fine family-style dish with considerable appeal.*

6 to 8 red sweet peppers
½ pound fillet of raw sole or flounder, ground or chopped fine
1 teaspoon coriander
¼ teaspoon ground cumin
2 kemiri nuts, crushed
½ cup fresh-grated coconut
2 eggs, beaten
1 tablespoon chopped celery leaves
2 scallions, chopped fine
1 teaspoon salt
2 teaspoons lemon juice
2 tablespoons cornstarch
½ cup peanut or corn oil

1. Cut the peppers in half, and remove the seeds and fibers.

2. For the filling, mix together the fish, coriander, cumin, kemiri, coconut, eggs, celery leaves, scallions, salt, lemon juice and cornstarch. Stuff each half pepper with the fish mixture.

3. Fry the peppers in the oil over medium heat, pepper side down, for about three minutes. Turn over, and brown the fish side for three minutes more. Drain on paper towels. Eat hot or cold.

Serves 6, with other dishes

Garnishes

Brambang Goreng
CRISPY FRIED ONIONS
(ALL INDONESIA)

Crispy onions are decorative and add flavor to a variety of vegetable, meat and rice dishes. They are deceptively simple to make, and one of the traditional stories concerns the classic confrontation of a mother-in-law with her prospective daughter-in-law who has burned the onions. It goes something like this: "What! How can you be a good wife to my son when you cannot even fry onions without burning them!"

1 cup thin-sliced small onions
½ teaspoon salt
½ cup peanut or corn oil

1. Sprinkle the onions with salt, mix well and let them stand for five minutes.

2. Turn out the onions on a paper or cloth towel, and squeeze the liquid out gently.

3. Heat the oil in a wok over a medium/low flame, and fry the onions for five to seven minutes, stirring frequently so that they will brown slowly and evenly. When they are light brown, remove them quickly from the oil, and drain them for fifteen minutes on paper towels. The onions will become crispy and darken somewhat. Store the onions at room temperature in a

jar with a tight cover or keep them in the freezer to be used when needed.

Makes about ½ cup

Bawang Puteh Goreng

CRISPY FRIED GARLIC SLICES

(ALL INDONESIA)

The garlic slices are used, along with the crispy fried onions, to garnish rice or anything else. They add dimension to rice, noodles or meats and are continuously useful to have around.

½ cup peanut or corn oil
10 or more cloves garlic

1. Heat the oil in a wok over a medium/low flame.
2. Cut the garlic vertically into thin slices.
3. Fry the garlic slices in oil until light brown. Turn out quickly on paper towels, and allow to drain for fifteen minutes. The crisp slices can be stored on the pantry shelf in a jar with a tight cover, or they can be frozen.

Makes ¼ cup

Serundeng Kacang
COCONUT CRUMBS WITH PEANUTS
(JAVA)

Serundeng *is a delicious adjunct to any* rijsttafel. *Easy to assemble and prepare, it can be made in a double recipe and stored for a considerable length of time in a jar with a tight cover. The roasted crumbs are sprinkled liberally on rice dishes to provide flavor and texture.*

A bonus is that the Serundeng *is compatible with Indian curry dishes.*

3 cloves garlic, sliced
2 tablespoons sliced onion
2 tablespoons sugar
1 teaspoon salt
1 teaspoon tamarind, dissolved in 2 teaspoons water
2 cups fresh-grated coconut
2 tablespoons peanut or corn oil
1 cup roasted peanuts, broken into quarters

1. In a mortar, crush the garlic, onion, sugar, salt and tamarind liquid into a paste. Mix with the grated coconut.

2. Heat the oil in a large frying pan, and toast the coconut mixture slowly over low heat, stirring frequently. When the mixture is nearly dry and light brown in color, about twenty minutes, add the peanuts, and toast for five minutes more. Allow the mixture to cool before storing.

Makes about 2½ cups

❂

Serundeng
BAKED SPICED COCONUT CRUMBS
(JAVA)

Like all garnishes of this type, the Serundeng *is sprinkled on rice dishes.*

2 cups fresh-grated coconut
1 tablespoon coriander
¼ teaspoon ground cumin
1 clove garlic, crushed
2 teaspoons sugar
1 teaspoon salt
2 teaspoons tamarind, dissolved in 1 tablespoon water
1 salam leaf
½ cup dry roasted soybeans

Aluminum foil

1. Line a cookie tray with aluminum foil. Mix together all the ingredients except the soybeans, and pour them into the tray.

2. Bake in a 250-degree oven for thirty minutes; stir frequently until light brown. Then add the soybeans, turn off the heat and continue to dry in the oven for thirty minutes more. Store in a jar with a tight cover.

Variation: Roast the coconut mixture in a frying pan over very low heat on top of the stove. Stir frequently for twenty to twenty-five minutes, or until the coconut is a light brown color. Add the soybeans, and toast for five minutes more.

Makes about 2 cups

Ebbi
DRIED SHRIMP FLAKES
(JAVA)

Ebbi *is a unique nutlike garnish with shrimpy overtones that can enrich any Indonesian meal. The shrimp flakes are used as a garnish on rice. They can be stored in a tightly covered jar on the pantry shelf for long periods of time. I have found it very convenient to keep a jar of the toasted flakes in the freezer and warm the estimated amount to be used. I urge the* rijsttafel *enthusiast to keep a quantity on hand.*

1 cup dried shrimp
1 cup water
2 teaspoons sugar
2 cloves garlic, crushed
½ teaspoon salt
1 teaspoon tamarind, soaked in 1 tablespoon water
2 tablespoons peanut or corn oil

1. Soak the shrimp in the water for one hour. The shrimp will swell and soften. Drain, and process in a blender a few at a time to flake coarsely.

2. Mix the shrimp flakes with the sugar, garlic, salt and

tamarind liquid. Add the oil to a frying pan, and over very low heat toast the shrimp mixture slowly for about thirty minutes, or until the flakes are light brown and dry. Cool and store.

Makes about ¾ cup

Several Ways with Eggs

Eggs are expensive in Indonesia and so are used sparingly. Both chicken and duck eggs can be used.

Risolles Solo
STUFFED EGG PANCAKES
(CENTRAL JAVA)

Risolles, *of Dutch Colonial origin, have been spiced in the Indonesian manner and integrated into the mainstream. It in no way diminishes a recipe to specify its European antecedents. On the contrary, I congratulate the flexibility with which the*

Indonesians have enlarged the scope and variety of their cuisine without the loss of identity.

THE FILLING:

¾ pound ground beef
¼ teaspoon pepper
1 teaspoon salt
1 teaspoon sugar
¼ teaspoon nutmeg
¼ cup carrot, cut into ⅛-inch square dice
1 tablespoon butter
1 tablespoon wheat flour, dissolved in 2 tablespoons water

THE PANCAKE:

2 eggs, beaten
1 cup flour
½ teaspoon salt
½ cup milk
½ cup plus 1 tablespoon cold water
Butter

THE STUFFED PANCAKE:

1 egg white, lightly beaten
3 tablespoons or more fine bread crumbs (optional)
2 tablespoons butter

1. Fry the beef, pepper, 1 teaspoon salt, sugar, nutmeg and carrot in the 1 tablespoon butter for about three or four minutes, or until the beef is cooked. Add the wheat flour paste, and mix well.

2. Mix the eggs, flour, ½ teaspoon salt, milk and water into

a smooth batter. Butter a crêpe pan, add 3 tablespoons batter and over medium/low heat brown the pancake lightly on both sides. Remove to a towel, and cool. Continue to make the crêpes until all the batter is used. This recipe makes about 12 crêpes.

3. Place 2 tablespoons of the beef filling in the center of a crêpe. Fold in the sides, and roll over to make a stuffed pancake 3 inches long and 1½ inches wide. Seal the ends with a dab of egg white. Continue to stuff all the crêpes with the beef mixture.

4. Butter a pan generously. Dip a stuffed pancake into the egg white, roll it lightly in the bread crumbs and brown it in butter over medium heat. Should one prefer not to use the bread crumbs, simply brown the crêpe on both sides in the butter.

The stuffed pancakes freeze very well. I would recommend that they be removed from the freezer one hour prior to being reheated for a minute or two under a broiler.

Another method is to freeze the *Risolles* after they have been stuffed but *before* they are fried. These should also be allowed to thaw out for one hour before they are fried in butter.

Serves 6

❁

Telor Bumbu Bali
SPICED EGGS
(BALI)

The red sweet pepper combined with dried red hot chili and the assertive seasoning of sweet soy sauce, tamarind and shrimp paste produces a red sweet and pungent sauce that elevates hard-cooked eggs to a new plateau. They will make an admirable addition to any rijsttafel.

- ***5 hard-boiled eggs, peeled***
- ***5 tablespoons peanut or corn oil***
- ***2 cloves garlic, sliced***
- ***¼ cup sliced onion***
- ***1 red sweet pepper, sliced***
- ***1 teaspoon dried red hot chili***
- ***¼ teaspoon shrimp (sauce) paste (see page 13)***
- ***½ cup water***
- ***1 teaspoon salt***
- ***½ teaspoon sugar***
- ***1 teaspoon tamarind, dissolved in 1 tablespoon water***
- ***2 teaspoons sweet soy sauce (see page 237)***
- ***1 slice ginger (about 1 teaspoon)***

1. Fry the eggs in 4 tablespoons of the oil for about five minutes, or until brown. Remove from the oil, and set aside.

2. Prepare the Bali sauce by blending the garlic, onion, sweet pepper, hot chili, shrimp paste and water into a fairly smooth

paste. Fry the sauce in the remaining 1 tablespoon oil for two minutes; then add the salt, sugar, tamarind liquid, sweet soy sauce and ginger. Add the eggs, and cook, basting frequently for five minutes more, or until the sauce is quite thick. To serve, cut the eggs in half lengthwise, and return to the sauce.

Serves 5, with other dishes

Sambal Goreng Telor

SPICED EGGS IN COCONUT SAUCE

(JAKARTA, JAVA)

- 5 *hard-boiled eggs, peeled*
- 2 *tablespoons peanut or corn oil*
- 1 *clove garlic, sliced thin*
- ¼ *cup thin-sliced onion*
- ½ *a fresh semihot chili, sliced thin*
- 1 *teaspoon tamarind, dissolved in 1 tablespoon water*
- ½ *teaspoon salt*
- ½ *teaspoon sugar*
- 1 *salam leaf*
- 1 *piece of laos*
- 1 *cup coconut milk (see page 15)*
- ¼ *teaspoon shrimp (sauce) paste (see page 13)*
- 1 *ripe tomato, cubed*

1. Fry the eggs in the oil for about five minutes, or until brown. Remove, and set aside.

2. Fry the garlic, onion and chili in the same oil for two

minutes. Add the eggs, tamarind liquid, salt, sugar, salam, laos, coconut milk and shrimp paste. Cook over medium heat for ten minutes, basting frequently.

3. Add the tomato, and cook for five minutes more. The sauce will have reduced by half and thickened. Serve hot or at room temperature.

Serves 5, with other dishes

Tahu Telor
SOYBEAN CAKE OMELET
(JAVA)

- ***2 Chinese soybean cakes, cut into 1-inch cubes***
- ***3 eggs***
- ***¼ teaspoon salt***
- ***2 tablespoons peanut or corn oil***

1. Dry the bean cake cubes on a towel. Beat the eggs, and add the salt and bean cake cubes.

2. Heat the oil in a frying pan, pour in the egg mixture and fry for about two minutes, or until just set. Fold the omelet in half, and fry until brown on both sides. This is a well-cooked omelet in the Indonesian manner. Serve with peanut butter sauce (page 240).

Makes 1 omelet

❁

Dadar Kepiting
CRAB MEAT OMELET
(SIDOARJO, JAVA)

Sidoarjo is a river port in East Java famous for the variety and quality of its seafood dishes. Crab omelet is one of the specialties of the town.

- ***¾ cup flaked fresh or canned crab meat***
- ***4 eggs, beaten***
- ***½ a fresh red hot chili, chopped***
- ***1 clove garlic, crushed***
- ***1 teaspoon salt***
- ***2 scallions, chopped***
- ***2 tablespoons peanut or corn oil***

1. Mix the crab meat, eggs, chili, garlic, salt and scallions together.

2. Heat the oil in a frying pan over medium heat. Add the egg mixture, and fry until just set. Turn over one end of the omelet slowly; delay a moment; then turn again into a roll. Turn again, and continue to fry until both sides of the omelet roll are firm. The shape should be an oblong, oval roll that is well done. Served hot or at room temperature.

Makes 1 omelet

Sauces and Dips

Kecap Manis
SWEET SOY SAUCE
(ALL INDONESIA)

Sweet soy is the most important sauce in the Indonesian repertoire. It is used as an indispensable seasoning in a great variety of dishes. The homemade sauce based on this recipe is infinitely superior to the store-bought brands found in Chinese and Southeast Asian food shops.

2½ cups sugar
1 bottle Chinese dark soy sauce (21 ounces equals about 2¾ cups)
3 cloves garlic, cracked
½ teaspoon star anise pods
2 salam leaves
2 pieces of laos
½ cup water

1. Carmelize the sugar in a saucepan over low heat, stirring frequently. When the sugar has melted, add the soy sauce and all the other ingredients.

2. Bring to a boil, and stir until the sugar has dissolved completely. Cook over low heat for ten minutes.

3. Allow this somewhat-thickened syrup to cool, and pour it into one or more bottles. I do not strain the sauce as I believe the garlic, anise, salam and laos continue to provide flavor. Sweet soy sauce keeps for several months refrigerated.
Makes about 2¾ cups

Sambal Kacang
PEANUT SAUCE—A DIP
(ALL INDONESIA)

Peanuts are a puzzle in the Indonesian kitchen. How did this legume, not a nut at all, travel from its historic origins in both Brazil and Africa to arrive at its indispensable position as the backbone of the satay, *the Indonesian national barbecue? Who introduced the peanut or groundnut or monkey nut (African nomenclature) to Indonesia; what routes did it take geographically and agriculturally before it became established in the archipelago? What adventurous cook invented the peanut sauces without which the island dishes would now be unthinkable?*

*The peanut (*Arachis hypogaea*) is an agricultural curiosity that arose apparently simultaneously in Africa and South America. This phenomenon has been explained by the continental drift that pushed the two continents apart. It is arguable that the Portuguese connection with Brazil was responsible for taking the peanut to Indonesia during their colonial expansion in Southeast Asia. It should also be noted, however, that the enduring influence of Hindu-Buddhist India on the cuisine of Indonesia, and India's own extraordinary preoccupation with the peanut—as the world's largest producer—must also provide an explanation for its movement from one continent to another.*

1 clove garlic, crushed
1 tablespoon peanut or corn oil
1 cup water
1 teaspoon dried hot red chili, soaked in 1 tablespoon water for thirty minutes
2 teaspoons tamarind, dissolved in 2 tablespoons water
½ teaspoon salt
1 to 2 tablespoons sugar, to taste
¼ teaspoon shrimp (sauce) paste (see page 13)
1 cup smooth or crunchy peanut butter

Fry the garlic in the oil for one minute. Add the water, chili, tamarind liquid, salt, sugar and shrimp paste. When the mixture starts to simmer, add the peanut butter, and stir until well blended. Allow the sauce to simmer for about five minutes,

stirring frequently. If it becomes too thick and unwieldy, add 1 or 2 tablespoons water. This dip is used with the classic chicken and beef *satays*. It can be stored in the refrigerator several days and reheated. It is eaten warm or hot.
Makes about 2 cups

Sambal Kacang
PEANUT BUTTER SAUCE
(JAVA)

This simple sauce is traditionally served with the Tahu Telor *(page 235).*

- *2 tablespoons crunchy peanut butter*
- *2 tablespoons water*
- *4 tablespoons sweet soy sauce (see page 237)*
- *1 clove garlic, crushed*
- *2 teaspoons lemon juice or 2 teaspoons tamarind dissolved in 2 tablespoons water*
- *2 teaspoons sugar*
- *2 teaspoons crushed dried red hot chili*

Stir the peanut butter and water into a paste. Add all the other ingredients, and mix well.
Makes about ½ cup

❁

Sambal Ulek Tomat
HOT TOMATO PASTE
(JAVA)

This fresh, hot paste is served frequently as a condiment with meat and fish dishes. I am partial to the Sambal Ulek *as a seasoning in any of the Indonesian soups.*

½ teaspoon salt
1 teaspoon shrimp (sauce) paste (see page 13)
½ teaspoon sugar
2 fresh green hot chilis, sliced thin
½ cup cubed ripe tomato

1. Crush the salt, shrimp paste, sugar and chilis in a mortar to produce a coarse paste.

2. Fold in the tomato cubes, and crush slightly to blend the flavors.

Makes about ½ cup

Sambal Kemiri
KEMIRI NUT PASTE
(JAVA)

This hot sour nut paste is a traditional accompaniment to Soto Ayam *(page 45) and* Soto Babat *(page 52)*.

- ***2 kemiri nuts***
- ***2 tablespoons lemon juice***
- ***1 tablespoon chopped onion***
- ***½ teaspoon salt***
- ***1 teaspoon dried or fresh hot red chili***

Crush all the ingredients together in a mortar. Mix well.

Note: Kemiri nuts are not always easy to come by. Unsalted macadamia nuts are a legitimate substitution if you double the required quantity.

Makes 2 to 3 tablespoons

❁

Sambal Badjak
PIRATE'S HOT PASTE
(EAST JAVA)

It has been said that in the early colonial days pirates prepared this fiery, hot condiment (Sambal) *to take with them as they plied their trade around the many islands of the Indonesian archipelago. It has now reached the shores of Brooklyn and been welcomed.*

1 cup dried red hot chili, soaked in 1 cup of water for one hour
2 tablespoons sliced onion
3 cloves garlic, sliced
1 teaspoon shrimp (sauce) paste (see page 13)
2 teaspoons salt
1 tablespoon sugar
1 teaspoon tamarind, dissolved in 1 tablespoon water
2 tablespoons butter
1 salam leaf

1. Put the chili with its soaking water, the onion, garlic, shrimp paste, salt, sugar and tamarind liquid in a blender, and prepare a coarse paste.

2. Put the butter in a saucepan, and add the chili paste and salam leaf. Cook the mixture over a medium low flame for about ten minutes, or until the liquid has evaporated.

The result is a thick hot paste that can be refrigerated for

some weeks. I have also stored the *Sambal* in the freezer for indefinite periods.
Makes about 1 cup

❁

Sambal Tomat
SWEET AND SOUR TOMATO DRESSING
(SOERABAJA, JAVA)

This dressing can be eaten with the various fritters, stuffed and plain (see page 202). Its use is similar to that of the American tomato ketchup.

1 cup sliced ripe tomatoes
1 clove garlic, sliced
1 tablespoon crushed dried red hot chili
1 teaspoon vinegar
1 teaspoon sugar
1 teaspoon salt
1/4 cup water
2 teaspoons peanut or corn oil

Blend the tomatoes, garlic, chili, vinegar, sugar, salt and water into a coarse paste. Fry the paste in the oil over low heat until the liquid is about half evaporated and a thick sauce remains.
Makes about ½ cup

Sweets

Indonesian desserts are, for the most part, the many varieties of fruit found in tropical countries, where the richness of the soil produces natural sugars that can be plucked ripe from the tree or plant. There are, however, some sweets rich in the Indonesian tradition that can be eaten with coffee or tea at any hour, or as dessert.

❁

Klepon
SWEET COCONUT RICE BALLS
(MADURA)

Klepon *is a specialty of the island of Madura. The green vegetable dye is made from the juice of the leaves of the pandanus tree.*

***1½ cups glutinous rice powder** (**see note page 247**)*
¾ cup lukewarm water
***2 drops green food coloring** (**optional**)*
***8 teaspoons dark brown sugar** (**approximately**)*
1 cup fresh-grated coconut, mixed with ½ teaspoon salt

1. Mix the rice powder, lukewarm water and green food coloring into a firm but flexible dough.

2. Pull off a heaping teaspoon of the dough, and shape a ball 1 inch in diameter. Push a finger into the center of the ball to make a well, and put in ¼ teaspoon of the brown sugar. Seal, and roll into a ball with the palms of the hands. Prepare all the balls, and set aside.

3. Drop the rice balls, three at a time, into a pot of boiling water, and cook for two minutes, or until the balls float to the surface. Remove them with a slotted spoon, and roll them in the grated coconut. The sugar will have dissolved inside. Serve at room temperature.

Makes about 30 rice balls

❁

Nagasari
STEAMED PLANTAIN DUMPLINGS
(SOERABAJA, JAVA)

All plantains are bananas, but not all bananas are plantains. Plantains are a variety of banana that are to be cooked, whereas bananas are generally eaten as an uncooked dessert. With this in mind, the unfamiliar texture of the Nagasari *should not discourage the adventurous cook. The ripe, sweet, bananalike flavor of the plantain is enhanced by the coconut-flavored gelatinous rice powder in which it is covered.*

Traditionally the Nagasari *is wrapped in banana leaves for steaming, and the rice paste is colored green with the juice of the leaf of the pandanus tree.*

1 cup glutinous rice powder (see below)
2 cups coconut milk (see page 15)
2 tablespoons brown or white sugar
1 very ripe black-skinned plantain

Seven 5-inch squares of aluminum foil

1. Dissolve the rice powder in ½ cup of the cool coconut milk to form a thick paste.

2. Bring the balance of the coconut milk (1½ cups) to a slow boil, add the sugar and mix well. Pour over the rice paste, and stir rapidly to a smooth, thick consistency.

Note: Glutinous rice powder can be purchased in 1-pound packages at all Southeast Asian food shops.

3. Cut the peeled plantain diagonally into ½-inch-thick slices. Place 1 heaping tablespoon rice paste in the center of a piece of foil, and top with a slice of plantain. Cover this with another tablespoon of paste. Smooth into a large egg-shaped oval. Fold over the four sides of the foil to make a square, and seal the ends of the package.

4. Steam the packages in a Chinese-style steamer for thirty minutes. Allow them to cool to room temperature, and remove the foil. The dumpling can also be cooled in the refrigerator and eaten chilled.

Makes 7 dumplings

Godok Godok
MASHED BANANA FRITTERS
(SUMATRA)

Godok Godok *is essentially a dessert and can be served as one, but I have discovered that for Western tastes, it also goes admirably with spicy Indonesian meat and fish dishes.*

- **5 *ripe bananas (about 2 pounds)***
- **1½ *cups rice flour***
- **2 *tablespoons dark or light brown sugar***
- **¼ *teaspoon salt***
- **½ *cup peanut or corn oil***

1. Mash the bananas, and mix with the rice flour, brown sugar and salt into a thick mélange.

2. Heat the oil in a wok or frying pan. Drop in 1 heaping

tablespoon of the banana mixture, and fry for about two minutes on each side. The fritters should be golden brown, soft and smoothly chewy. Drain on paper towels, and serve hot or at room temperature.

Makes about 20 fritters

❁

Sri Kaya Pisang

STEAMED PLANTAIN CUSTARD

(JAVA)

2 eggs
3 tablespoons sugar
1½ cups coconut milk (see page 15)
A pinch of salt
½-inch cinnamon stick
2 whole cloves
1 ripe black-skinned plantain

1. Beat the eggs and sugar together until lemon yellow. Add the coconut milk, salt, cinnamon and cloves. Pour into a heatproof dish.

2. Peel the plantain, and cut diagonally into ½-inch-thick slices. Distribute the slices in the egg mixture.

3. Steam in a Chinese-style steamer for thirty minutes. Serve the custard hot.

Serves 6

Getuk

SWEET POTATO CAKE WITH COCONUT

(SOLO, JAVA)

This is a popular breakfast dish eaten with coffee in the city of Solo. Vendors hawk Getuk *to employees of commercial firms who take their breakfast break with this sweet and nourishing concoction.*

1 pound sweet potatoes
2 teaspoons sugar
A drop of vanilla (optional)
1 cup fresh-grated coconut, mixed with 1 teaspoon salt

1. Boil the sweet potatoes in water until soft. Drain well. Mash, and add the sugar, vanilla and ½ cup of the grated coconut.

2. Mold the sweet potato mixture in a small, round soup plate. Turn the *Getuk* onto a serving platter, and sprinkle with the remaining ½ cup coconut. Serve at room temperature, or refrigerate for one hour and serve chilled.

Serves 6

❁

Dadar Guling
STUFFED ROLLING PANCAKES
(CENTRAL JAVA)

Sugar is the variable factor in seasoning the coconut stuffing. The Javanese, with their seemingly enormous capacity for sweets, would sweeten the coconut as indicated in the recipe. You may wish to reduce the brown sugar or eliminate the white sugar entirely.

THE STUFFING:

- *2 cups fresh-grated coconut*
- *10 tablespoons dark or light brown sugar*
- *1 tablespoon white sugar*
- *1 3-inch cinnamon stick, broken in half*
- *¼ teaspoon salt*

THE PANCAKE:

- *1 cup rice flour*
- *½ cup cornstarch*
- *1¾ cups coconut milk (see page 15)*
- *½ teaspoon salt*
- *1 egg, beaten*
- *Peanut or corn oil*

1. *The Stuffing:* Mix the grated coconut, brown and white sugars, cinnamon and ¼ teaspoon salt together. Fry the mixture in a dry pan over medium/low heat, stirring constantly, for five

minutes, or until the mixture is dry. Remove the cinnamon stick, and set aside.

2. *The Pancake:* Mix the rice flour, cornstarch, coconut milk, ½ teaspoon salt and egg into a smooth batter. Lightly oil an 8-inch frying pan, and pour 3 tablespoons of the batter into the pan, covering it with a thin layer. Fry for one minute, turn the pancake over and fry for one minute on the other side. Remove, and set aside.

3. *The Dessert:* Place 2 tablespoons of the coconut mixture on the near edge of the pancake. Fold over once, then tuck in the left and right sides and fold over once more. Press gently to distribute the coconut evenly. Serve at room temperature.

Makes 10 to 12 stuffed pancakes

❁

Ketan Juruh

COCONUT SWEET RICE

(SOLO, JAVA)

2 cups well-washed glutinous rice (see page 18)
2 cups coconut milk (see page 15)
1 cup dark brown sugar
¼ cup water
A pinch of salt
⅛ teaspoon vanilla
½ cup fresh-grated coconut

Aluminum foil

1. In a saucepan, bring the rice and coconut milk to a boil, stir several times and turn off the heat. Let stand for fifteen minutes to allow the rice to absorb the milk. Then pile the rice on aluminum foil in a Chinese-style steamer, and steam for twenty minutes.

2. Make a fairly thick syrup by cooking the brown sugar, water, salt and vanilla in a saucepan over medium/low flame for ten minutes.

3. To serve, place a mound (½ cup) of the rice on a plate. Scatter 1 heaping tablespoon grated coconut over the rice, and dribble 1 tablespoon syrup over all. If you have a sweet tooth, add more syrup. Serve at room temperature.

Serves 6

Pisang Goreng
FRIED PLANTAIN
(JAVA)

The ripe plantain is a versatile fruit/vegetable that is used in many cultures. I like the Indonesian way since it may be eaten hot or at room temperature, as a dessert or as a side dish with meat and rice dishes.

1 ripe black-skinned plantain
1 egg
1 teaspoon sugar
6 tablespoons flour
A pinch of salt
2 tablespoons coconut milk (see page 15) or water
2 drops vanilla (optional)
¼ cup peanut or corn oil

1. Cut the peeled plantain diagonally into ½-inch-thick slices.
2. Make a batter of the egg, sugar, flour, salt, coconut milk and vanilla if used.
3. Heat the oil in a frying pan over medium heat. Dip the plantain slices in the batter, and fry them until golden brown on both sides. Drain on paper towels.

Variation: Fresh or canned pineapple, cut to approximately the same size as the plantain, may be used to good advantage. Dip the pineapple into the batter, and brown on all sides in the oil.

Serves 4, with other dishes

Kolak

TAPIOCA AND PLANTAIN DESSERT

(SUMATRA)

The cassava root is what we are concerned with here, although the Sumatrans refer to the plant as tapioca. In reality, the tapioca granules used in European types of desserts are derived from the cassava. The cassava is one of the starchy roots seen frequently in Latin American shops.

1 pound tapioca root, peeled and cut into ½-inch cubes
½ cup water
¼ cup light or dark brown sugar
2 ripe black-skinned plantains
¼ teaspoon vanilla
1½ cups coconut milk (see page 15)
1 tablespoon white sugar

One 1-inch cinnamon stick (optional)

Cook the tapioca cubes in the water and brown sugar for about thirty minutes, or until soft. The water will be almost completely evaporated. Add the plantain, cut into ½-inch-thick slices, the vanilla, coconut milk, white sugar and cinnamon if used. Cook for about fifteen minutes, or until the plantain is soft and the sauce has thickened. This thick stew can be enjoyed hot, cold or at room temperature.

Variation: The sweet potato can be substituted for the tapioca and the recipe followed as written.

Serves 8

How to Assemble a Rijsttafel, with Suggested Menus

The secret to preparing an Indonesian meal for two or twenty-two is compatibility. Since the repertory is large, and the variety comprehensive, one should choose carefully to fulfill the demands of personal preference while generously catering to the whims of guests. The sauces of black, red and gold; the crunchy, crispy, creamy and chewy textures and the hot, bitter, sweet, pungent and aromatic flavors, both sensual and filling, make the task of assembling a *rijsttafel* stimulating and exotic.

It is not difficult once the various techniques of the cuisine are mastered. Balancing a chili-hot dish against one that is mildly spiced or sweet will allow you to explore the tradition without being repetitious. Furthermore, as the number of diners increases, it is in keeping with the Indonesian idea of dining to add dishes in direct proportion to the increase in the numbers. Providing modest quantities of a variety of foods rather than large quantities of one dish will add to the excitement of discovery within the framework of the tradition.

Many dishes can be made a day or two in advance, and the flavors—especially of meats—are intensified by their being marinated in their sauces for a length of time and then reheated. Other dishes freeze well and can be prepared days or weeks in advance of a *rijsttafel* to simplify the preparation without sacrificing the quality or variety of the food. The American kitchen cannot rely on an apparently inexhaustible source of inexpensive household staff (as can be found in Asia), and for that reason each shortcut is to be welcomed.

Rice, both white and flavored, is ubiquitous on the Indonesian table, and a *rijsttafel* would be unthinkable without it. Generously served, it helps to dilute the intensity of a spicy cuisine without losing its identity. So one can begin to plan a meal with rice and then add the other dishes. A hot sauce, such as pirate's paste (page 243), the sweet soy sauce and the *krupuk* (page 203), should be considered standard menu items that will add to the gastronomic exotica of the *rijsttafel*. All the menus listed below should automatically include rice, a hot sauce, *krupuk* and the sweet soy sauce.

The Indonesian system of dining is an excellent way to provide proper nutritional balance. Moderation in dining is sensible, as well as medically recommended. When it is combined with the culinary balance and variety of an exotic cuisine, it would be difficult to challenge as a way of life.

The following suggested menus have been selected for their compatibility and interest. It should be noted that each basic menu is designed for two people, and dishes are added to accommodate a dinner for six or ten. Naturally, one can double the recipe of the important meat and vegetable dishes without overwhelming the idea of a traditional *rijsttafel*. The name of the game, however, is variety in modest but sufficient quantities.

Two Persons	*Six Persons*	*Ten Persons*
Rempah	Same	Same
Opor Ayam	Same	Same
Timor Acar	Same	Same
	Perkedel Ikan	Same
	Soerabaya	*Perkedel Jagung*
		Karangmenanci
Gado Gado	Same	Same
Ayam Goreng	Same	Same
	Asam Pade Daging	Same
		Sambal Goreng
		Udang
Martabak	Same	Same
Kare Ayam	Same	Same
	Orak Arik Jagung	Same
		Sambal Goreng
		Tomat
Bebek Bumbu Bali	Same	Same
Acar	Same	Same
	Terong Kari	Same
		Empal
Magadip	Same	Same
Sambal Goreng	Same	Same
Bung	*Telor Bumbu Bali*	Same
	Gimbal Udang	Same
		Sambal Goreng Ati

Two Persons	*Six Persons*	*Ten Persons*
Satay Pentul	Same	Same
Acar Kuning	Same	Same
	Oseng Oseng Jamur	Same Same
	Godok Godok	*Perkedel Kepiting*
		Sri Kaya Pisang

Spices as Medicinal Remedies

The craft of curing ailments with herbal medicines is as ancient as man himself. The twentieth century has not altered the practices of witch doctors, either quacks or those village people with a profound knowledge and confidence in the efficacy of roots, leaves and the medicinal essences that can be derived from them.

In countries all over the world, the village poor (and many wealthy believers) are dependent on herbs, spices and vegetable compounds to cure ailments both common and complex. Many spices and seasonings may originally have been used for their medicinal properties before being incorporated into the development of a cuisine. Domestic remedies that were in every household and probably kept in what could be considered the kitchen or cooking area became part of daily living in every sense of the word. We can only hypothesize as to what came first, curing or cooking. But how easy it must have been to move from one activity to the other!

During the heyday of the Portuguese, Spanish, Dutch and English colonial periods there was an insatiable European demand for spices to use not only in the cooking but also as therapy for the exotic (sometimes bizarre) medical complaints of the upper classes, who could afford the prices.

The following list of spices and seasonings used in the Indonesian kitchen and their pharmacological properties, according to Indonesian herbal specialists, are given below. One should not judge or ridicule the alleged miracles that spices can perform. Modern medicine has in many cases used the herbal cures as a guide to chemical synthesis. The English name for each precedes the Indonesian name.

1. **Cardamom, *kapulaga:*** cough, tonsilitis, upset stomach, dysmenorrhea, stomach spasm, itching throat, stomach disturbances, influenza, asthma, fatigue, fever, body odor.

2. **Chili, *cabe/lombok:*** contains vitamins A, C and P (citrin), for scabies, pimples, stomach ache, loss of appetite, low blood pressure.

3. **Cinnamon, *kayu manis jangan:*** apathy, eczema, rheumatism, high blood pressure, vomiting, asthma, colds, diarrhea, cough.

4. **Citrus leaves, *jeruk purut:*** care of hair, dandruff, fatigue, influenza (both the leaves and juice of the fruit are used for this).

5. **Cloves, *cengkeh:*** colds, coughs, toothache, stomach disturbances, low sensual desire.

6. **Coriander, *ketumbar:*** stomach disturbances, headache, digestion, apathy, regular menstruation.

7. **Cumin, *jientan:*** diphtheria, stomach disturbances, rheuma-

tism, tetanus, trachoma, poisonous insect bites, food allergies, ear infections, coughs, fever, influenza.

8. **Garlic, *bawang putih:*** asthma, cough, vomiting, ear infections, itching, skin diseases, colds, bites of poisonous insects, high blood pressure, cholera, vermifuge (worms), migraine, painful menstruation, thorn prickle, low sensual desire.

9. **Ginger root, *jahe:*** poor appetite, digestion, headache, coughs, rheumatism, itching, cholera, snakebite, diphtheria, colds, vomiting, dislocation of joints, swellings.

10. **Kemiri nut:** contains stearin, fatty acids, protein, glycerin, phosphoric acid and vitamin B_1, for hair growth.

11. **Kencur root:** contains volatile oils, starch and minerals, for colds, inflammatory diseases of the mouth, cough, toothache, stomach ache, swellings, vomiting, stiff muscles, poisonous food.

12. **Kunci root (*Kaemferia pandurata*):** contains iron, vitamins A and C, for apathy, colds, puerperal fever, itching, coughs, worms, upset stomach, slow urination, pain in bladder, skin diseases.

13. **Laos root, *laos/lengkuas:*** eczema, bronchitis, colds, skin diseases, ear infections, stomach disturbances, pain, scabies, cholera.

14. **Lemon grass, *sereh:*** irregular menstruation, better perspiration, increase of appetite, swollen gums, colds, dislocation of joints, cholera, vomiting, rheumatism, stomach and bowel infections.

15. **Nutmeg, *pala:*** apathy, stomach spasms, ear infections, low sensual desire, low blood pressure, vomiting, rheumatism.

16. **Onion, *bawang merah:*** coughs, colds, vomiting, convulsions, apathy, pox, swellings, fever.

17. **Pepper, *merica/lada:*** improved menstruation, asthma, colds, influenza, fever, low blood pressure.

18. **Salam leaves, *daun salam:*** contains volatile oils, for diarrhea and weak stomach.

19. **Tamarind, *asem:*** contains vitamins A, B_1 and C, for rheumatism, wounds, skin diseases, breast infections, fever, apathy, eczema, diarrhea, pimples, pox, skin eruptions, nervousness.

20. **Turmeric, *kunyit/kunir:*** dysentery, diarrhea, uteritis, tonsilitis, asthma, wounds and cuts, itching, gum infections, swellings, scabies, nasal infections, trachoma, eczema and anemia.

Glossary of Ingredients with Latin Names

1. **Capsicum** chili (*Capsicum annum,* mild, and *Capsicum frutescens,* hot)
2. **Cinnamon** (*Cinnamomum zeylanicum*)
3. **Clove** (*Syzgium aromaticum*)
4. **Coconut** (*Cocos nucifera*)
5. **Cumin** (*Cuminum cyminum*)
6. **Coriander** (*Coriandrum sativum*)
7. **Chinese cabbage** (*Brassica pekinensis*)
8. **Garlic** (*Allium sativum*)
9. **Ginger** (*Zingiber officinale*)
10. **Jeruk purut,** papeda or citron (*Citrus hystrix*)
11. **Kemiri,** candlenut, tung nut, country walnut (*Aleurites triloba*)
12. **Kencur** (*Cemeheria galanga*)
13. **Laos,** a type of ginger root (*Alpinea galanga*)
14. **Malinjo** (*Gnetum gnemom*)

15. **Macadamia** or Queensland nut (*Macadamia ternifolia*)
16. **Nutmeg** (*Myristica fragrans*)
17. **Onion** (*Allium cepa*)
18. **Pare,** bitter melon, bitter gourd or balsam pear (*Momordica charantia*)
19. **Pepper** (*Liper nigrum*)
20. **Salam,** laurel leaf (*Eugeneia polyanza*)
21. **Peanut,** groundnut or monkey nut (*Arachus hypogaea*)
22. **Kacang Panjang,** long Chinese string bean (*Phaseolus vulgaris*)
23. **Shallot** (*Allium cepa* of the Aggregatum group)
24. **Sereh,** lemon grass (*Cymbopogon citratus*)
25. **Tamarind** (*Tamarindus indica*)
26. **Turmeric** (*Curcuma longa*)

REFERENCES:

Harrison, S. G., G. B. Masefield, Michael Wallis, *The Oxford Book of Food Plants*. New York: Oxford University Press, 1969.

Macmillan, H. F., *Tropical Planting & Gardening*. London: Macmillan & Co., 1956.

Index

A textile importer who lives in Brooklyn Heights, *Copeland Marks* has traveled extensively in Indonesia, searching for handicrafts and, incidentally, studying the native cuisine. His writing about Indonesian food has appeared in *Gourmet* and other magazines. Co-author *Mintari Soeharjo* is Indonesian, a native of Central Java where she continues to maintain her home.